On the Ash Heap With No Answers

IVERNA TOMPKINS
with JUDSON CORNWALL

CREATION
HOUSE
Lake Mary, Florida

Creation House
Strang Communications Company
600 Rinehart Road
Lake Mary, FL 32746
(407) 333-0600

To my entire staff—
teachers, office workers and faithful volunteers
who labor with me to train leaders to train others

ACKNOWLEDGMENT

Thanks to my brother Judson for adding to his already full schedule the task of putting my thoughts and preaching into readable form so I could share this book with you.

CONTENTS

PREFACE

For centuries the book of Job has encouraged believers as they suffered — having no ready explanation for their families and friends as to the reason for the suffering or why healing didn't happen immediately.

But does the book of Job have another application for the body of Christ? Reading it again, I saw the comfort God provided for Job as he lived through his unexplained tragedies. This comfort was sent by way of four friends, obviously touched with Job's feelings. They sat in silence to lend strength of support by just being there. But as God stirred in these men a reminder of His greatness, holiness and faithfulness, each one concluded that Job must be concealing sin; why else would a holy, faithful, wise God allow Job to suffer such losses? In these conclusions the prophetic insight became tainted. When the prophetic word came through these men, it was no longer a word of comfort but a condemnation of Job. No words except the description of God could encourage or build Job up. His friends spoke those words, but Job missed their comfort because he was busy defending his innocence.

Today, with such an emphasis being placed on the prophetic ministry, I believe we can learn much from the book of Job — about giving and receiving a prophetic word.

Since the book of Job is not as frequently read as the Psalter, I recommend that you refresh your mind by reading it again before reading this book. Keeping a copy of Job close will make this book even more valuable.

Iverna Tompkins
Scottsdale, Arizona
January 1992

ONE

RELATING
TO PROPHECY
AND PROPHETS

It was a time in history that cannot be repeated. The
earth was underpopulated. Ecology was in perfect
balance. Smog never darkened the skies, and the
rivers, lakes and oceans sparkled with crystal-pure water.
The family was the center of government. The culture
was pastoral. Cattle, camels and children were the standard measurement of wealth. By present standards life
was simple, almost simplistic, and a two-hundred-year
life span was common.

These were the days in which wealthy Job lived. There
is nothing in this oldest book of the Bible that accurately
dates its central character, Job. But the few facts culled
from the narrative place him very close to the time of
Abraham.

These were the days before the written Bible. We call
it the patriarchal period. Abraham, Isaac and Jacob are
the best-known of the patriarchs, but Job was also among
them.

Consistent with Abraham's time, the social unit in
the book of Job is the patriarchal family-clan. There are
no references to Israel, the exodus, the Mosaic Law or
the tabernacle in the book of Job. Job offered sacrifices

as the priest of his family. Furthermore, Job used the distinctive patriarchal name for God thirty-one times — *Shaddai* (the Almighty). The rest of the Old Testament uses this name for God only seventeen times.

God Is a Speaking God

The Bible teaches us that Adam had fellowship with the voice of God. God spoke; Adam understood. It was the same with Noah, who experienced no angelic appearance or divine visitation. Noah merely heard the voice of God, understood it and obeyed.

Abraham, from Ur of Chaldea, seems to have been the first person after Noah to have heard and understood the voice of God; he had fellowship with God through the channel of conversation. So did Job, far off in another land — in Uz in the area of Edom. (Neither race nor culture matters to God.) But, for Job, hearing from God was a learned experience; the book of Job shows that he was a slow learner.

The first chapter of this ancient book speaks of Job's wealth, his family, his blamelessness and his uprightness. It declares that Job feared and worshipped God while faithfully shunning evil. But not once does it mention Job's having communication with God. God blessed Job, but it appears that this patriarch had not yet developed a capacity to hear the voice of God.

Yet through the course of the book of Job God continued to speak to Job — through assorted persons and finally directly.

Until the very last Job did not understand any of this. Job didn't recognize God. While consistently declaring his righteousness, Job cried mournfully,

Look, I go forward, but He is not there,
And backward, but I cannot perceive Him;
When He works on the left hand, I cannot
    behold Him;
When He turns to the right hand, I cannot
    see Him (23:8-9).

If Job could not have face-to-face communication with God, he refused to learn. Job wanted the words of God to come directly from God's mouth, while Jehovah chose to speak through trusted friends of Job. It is a case of the student refusing to pass a course because he or she dislikes the instructor.

The story of Job is about learning to hear God. While Abraham didn't seem to have any problem distinguishing God's voice, Job did. He eventually came to realize that hearing God is a learned art far more than a spiritual gift. In some ways Job exemplifies some of the persons to whom the book of Hebrews was written.

For though by this time you ought to be teachers, you need someone to teach you again the first principles of the oracles of God; and you have come to need milk and not solid food. For everyone who partakes only of milk is unskilled in the word of righteousness, for he is a babe. But solid food belongs to those who are of full age, that is, those who by reason of use have their senses exercised to discern both good and evil (Hebrews 5:12-14).

The Cast of Characters

The book of Job abounds with voices. It begins with the voice of the narrator, who remains anonymous. Starting at verse 6 we move from earth to heaven and listen in on a conversation between Jehovah and Satan. Then, returning to earth, we hear the voices of Job's servants bringing messages of disaster and gloom. The speaking voices multiply rapidly.

Although chapter 2 is short, it introduces four more speakers. Job's wife and his three friends come on the scene. Not until chapter 32 do we hear from a fourth friend, Elihu, and God speaks directly to Job in chapter 38. Perhaps we should be more sympathetic with Job's difficulty in hearing the message God was sending. So much speaking confused him.

Twentieth-Century Voices

If Job became confused because of the multiplicity of voices in his day, is it any wonder that modern Christians find it difficult to hear the voice of God? Voices bombard us beyond anything the world has ever seen. Radio, television, public address systems — our minds are assaulted in public places as well as in our homes.

Add to this the proliferation of the printed page, and the volume of voices through which we have to sift daily is overwhelming. Publishers print thousands of new books every year. Daily newspapers line our doorsteps, and junk mail clutters our mailboxes. Signs, billboards and other forms of publicity constantly stimulate the mind — unless one is climbing a mountain or lost in the desert. We are so mentally stimulated that it is difficult to hear our own spirits.

The earnest Christian who desires to hear what God is saying in this day faces further confusion that rivals the book of Job. In our generation a thousand outside voices have replaced the simplicity of believing the Bible as interpreted by the local pastor. These voices often contradict one another.

It has long been argued that the inability of religious denominations to agree on doctrine has been a deterrent to outsiders seeking spiritual help in American churches. If students of the Bible cannot agree on what it says, what chance is there for others to understand God's Word? Modern Christians may feel like Pilate at the trial of Jesus: "What is truth?" (John 18:38).

Truth Has Many Facets

While the many religious voices heard today may occasionally contradict one another, most are simply stating the truth from a personal perspective. None of us stands in a position that allows us to see the whole truth.

My studies in the book of Job have convinced me that the four friends of Job brought different aspects of truth to this godly man who was suffering.

It is popular to discredit the speeches of Job's friends because God rebuked them. This is surface interpretation. A closer look at what God said reveals that Jehovah reprimanded them for their condemning *application* of those messages. What they said about the nature of God was fundamentally correct. God intended those messages to encourage Job and to give some understanding to what he was experiencing.

For instance, Eliphaz told Job,

> Now acquaint yourself with Him, and be at
>   peace;
> Thereby good will come to you.
> Receive, please, instruction from His mouth,
> And lay up His words in your heart....
> Yes, the Almighty will be your gold
> And your precious silver;

> For then you will have your delight in the Al-
> mighty,
> And lift up your face to God (22:21-22, 25-
> 26).

Through this human channel God was reaching out to Job in a greater revelation of the divine than Job had ever known before.

Though each man came from his own place and had a different perspective, what they said collectively joined together like pieces of a jigsaw puzzle. No one piece formed the picture, but each revealed an aspect of God that could help Job through his difficulties. While not one of them had a full revelation of God, each contributed something that the others lacked. As Paul put it, "For we know in part and we prophesy in part" (1 Corinthians 13:9).

We can see this principle throughout the writings of the Old Testament prophets. No prophet has a full revelation of God. Isaiah burned with the concept of a holy God. Hosea spoke only of a wounded, loving God, while Amos called passionately for social justice. Jeremiah saw God's continuing judgments, while Ezekiel saw God's coming restoration. No one prophet displayed a true picture of God, but each had a valid concept. The Holy Spirit used each messenger as a color pigment on His palette as He painted a masterful portrait of a coming Redeemer named Jesus.

The same is true in the book of Job. The Holy Spirit used a great variety of voices, some of them in agreement and others proclaiming dissimilar thoughts. God used each voice to paint a picture of the sovereign *Shaddai* whom Job loved and served.

The Poetry of the Book of Job

I refer to God's revelation to Job as a painting, but in reality it is a poem. The poetry of the book is beautiful and sublime. The International Standard Bible Encyclopedia says, "The speeches, the bulk of the work, are composed in beautiful poetry that uses the richest variety of vocabulary and style found in the Old Testament." While something is always lost in the translation of poetry, even our English version of this book stands as a literary classic. The poetic portion of the book is a series of speeches. Each of the three friends speaks, and each speech is followed by a reply from Job. After the three older friends have spoken, the younger man, Elihu, shares what he knows about God, and then God comes on the scene to conclude the seminar. The speakers masterfully use images, figures of speech, similes and anecdotes to communicate the deep feelings of Job, the delicate but deliberate way they each try to change these feelings and the word of God Himself. This epic poem is a moving drama worthy of being played to the accompaniment of symphonic music. The Illustrated Bible Dictionary concludes, "We may regard it as one of the most original works in the poetry of mankind."

But it is more than this. The poem is a vehicle by which God communicates deep truths about Himself and His methods of self-revelation. While we habitually declare Job to be the subject of this book, God is more properly its theme. Job is merely subjected to the instruction of God.

Through Whom Can God Speak?

In a word the answer is *anybody*. Consider the strange story of Balaam and his donkey, found in Numbers 22.

God sometimes chooses a channel because of its availability, not because of its holiness.

Then there's the Old Testament story of the three Hebrew children thrown into a fiery furnace. They were joined by a fourth person in the fire. But the three boys didn't give testimony to the presence of the fourth. This observation came from Nebuchadnezzar, the king who had ordered them into the furnace. He testified:

> Blessed be the God of Shadrach, Meshach, and Abed-Nego, who sent His Angel and delivered His servants who trusted in Him, and they have frustrated the king's word, and yielded their bodies, that they should not serve nor worship any god except their own God! (Daniel 3:28).

Frequently the person in the furnace of affliction senses neither the presence nor the purposes of God. Sometimes I have been so aware of my pain that I have missed His presence. The inner turmoil and the outer turbulence made me so self-conscious that I didn't recognize the fresh revelation God was offering to me. This is why God often has an outsider looking on who can define what is happening and give glory to God for the process. God opens their eyes to see beyond the natural scheme of things. We call these observers and proclaimers *prophets*.

Just as many motorists listen to their car radios for the helicopter traffic report to help guide them around accidents or stalled traffic, Christians often need an outside observer who can view the situation from the top. When we are caught in, and often become a part of, the problem, we usually have tunnel vision. We need an outside perspective to give us the overview of what is happening.

This was God's promise to His covenant people. He said,

> Your eyes shall see your teachers.
> Your ears shall hear a word behind you, say-
> ing,
> "This is the way, walk in it,"
> Whenever you turn to the right hand
> Or whenever you turn to the left (Isaiah
> 30:21).

In the Old Testament this gifting of the prophets to see beyond the natural gave them the title of seers. They saw what others could not see, and the people anticipated that the prophets would faithfully tell them what they saw. There is a common assumption that prophecy is for the future. Sometimes it is, but since God lives in an eternal *now*, His word to us affects our present as well as our past and future. The confusion of everyday living with its myriad of decisions is overcome by a word from the Lord. Divine direction gives purpose to our activities and renews our courage. David seemed convinced that the voice of the Lord had a genuine involvement in daily living. He wrote:

> The voice of the Lord is over the waters;
> ...is powerful;
> ...splinters the cedars...
> ...divides the flames of fire.
> ...shakes the wilderness;
> ...makes the deer give birth,
> And strips the forests bare;
> And in His temple everyone says, "Glory!"
> (Psalm 29:3-9).

If God's voice is this involved in the daily course of nature, how much more involved is His voice in the lives of His saints?

16

God did not leave Job in his misery without observers who could see beyond the physical problems he was experiencing. Four of Job's friends, three of them contemporaries and the fourth a much younger man, came to him as comforters. Rich and affluent as Job had been, Eliphaz, Bildad and Zophar were members of the Wise. The Illustrated Bible Dictionary says, "The Wise in Israel sought to understand God and His ways by studying the great uniformities of human experience by reason illuminated by 'the fear of the Lord.' Proverbs is a typical example of their understanding of life."

Eliphaz the Temanite told Job,

> Yet man is born to trouble,
> As the sparks fly upward.
> But as for me, I would seek God,
> And to God I would commit my cause —
> Who does great things, and unsearchable,
> Marvelous things without number (5:7-9).

He saw God's greatness in contrast to man's frailty.

Similarly, Bildad the Shuhite sought to encourage Job from his observance of God in the world. He said,

> Behold, God will not cast away the blame-
>   less,
> Nor will He uphold the evildoers.
> He will yet fill your mouth with laughing,
> And your lips with rejoicing (8:20-21).

At times we need the voice of the seer — the prophet — to help us see beyond the obvious and to recognize the hand of God in our providential circumstances.

Through Whom Does God Usually Speak?

Throughout the Old Testament the people known as prophets were seldom strangers. Kings sent for them by name, and people sought them out for divine wisdom. They were holy men whose life-styles gave validity to their messages. Whether liked or disliked, they were known as channels through whom God frequently communicated His will.

There was great diversity among these prophets. Some lived the life of a recluse; others were family men. Some chose to live in the countryside; others were city dwellers. Some were peasants, and others, like Isaiah, were members of the royal court. It was not their dress, habits or life-styles that identified them as prophets. It was their consistent ministry backed up with holiness of character.

Prophecy, as I view it, is not merely the words spoken by a recognized prophet. Any communication from God to an individual is prophetic, whether it comes through a sermon, a book, a friend's conversation or a "thus saith the Lord."

Job's comforters were friends. How faithful of the Lord to speak through persons Job knew and trusted. These five men had built friendships when all was well. Job could lean safely on those relationships now when all seemed wrong, for

> A friend loves at all times,
> And a brother is born for adversity (Proverbs 17:17).

Job needed the wisdom of friends when he was wounded and confused. A wise man observed,

Ointment and perfume delight the heart,
And the sweetness of a man's friend does so
   by hearty counsel (Proverbs 27:9).

In the midst of his bitter agony Job needed the sweetness of his friend's counsel, even though some of what they said cut to the quick.

Paul wisely admonished the new converts in Thessalonica "to know them which labour among you, and are over you in the Lord, and admonish you" (1 Thessalonians 5:12, KJV). One of the joys of Christian fellowship is getting to know those people God has placed in the body for our edification, instruction and comfort. These interpersonal relationships build friendships that we need in times of adversity.

I have always found it comforting to know the prophet through whom God has communicated to me. Sometimes this knowledge gave me a better understanding of the message. Even if I could not understand some things said, I could trust this person's love for me and simply wait to see what came to pass.

There are other times, however, when close associates know too much of our personal circumstances to be a clear vessel through whom God can speak. Their emotional involvement and their deep love set up an unconscious censorship that hinders the flow of prophecy through them.

At times it seems easier to believe the word of the Lord when it comes through a person who knows nothing about me or my circumstances and yet speaks as if he or she does. This makes it more convincing that it is a word from God.

Many years ago when I was running from the ministry because I was weary of the "women be silent" accusations, I attended a World Map camp meeting. The speaker was David Shock. I had never met this man personally, and you can imagine my surprise when he stopped preaching and pointed to me, saying, "You, in the third row back, the third person in: Come down here!" I counted the seats and trembled as I made my way to the front.

He said to me, "God is sending you to the whole body of Christ. Not like you've known in the past — that was your school. There is a whole horn of oil about to be poured out on you. Don't ever ask for a meeting. Don't write a letter or make a phone call. God is going to open doors for you...."

I never doubted that God had spoken even though the word seemed impossible to be fulfilled. I knew David Shock didn't know of my dilemma — feeling the pull between my desire to fulfill God's calling and my anguish over being ridiculed as a woman in ministry. I have always done as God asked through the prophet, and there has never been a lack of places for me to minister.

If a friend who knew my circumstances had offered those words to me, I may have passed them off as sympathetic concern, so God spoke to me through a known prophet who was not known to me.

God may speak to us through persons known or unknown to us. God sends His word according to our needs. On occasion in the Bible total unknowns appeared on the scene with a word from Jehovah. Those who do not know us at all may not offer us much empathy, but their objectivity can be vital. But at times there is strength in knowing the vessels God uses in our lives. Those who know us will offer us empathy and family love. God sends them as a healing potion for our soul and spirit. God mercifully chose lifelong friends to talk to Job.

TWO

REASONS FOR PROPHECY

When the curtain rises on the drama of Job's life, he is a prosperous man: ten children, seven thousand sheep, three thousand camels, five hundred yoke of oxen — "the greatest of all the people of the East" (1:3).

As we'll see later, it seems that Job accepted physical blessings as evidence of God's approval of his life. He envisioned a spiritual merit system where the righteous were rewarded and the wicked punished. That it seemed to be working for him was evident even to Satan. When God asked him about Job,

> Satan answered the Lord and said, "Does Job fear God for nothing? Have You not made a hedge around him, around his household, and around all that he has on every side? You have blessed the work of his hands, and his possessions have increased in the land. But now, stretch out Your hand and touch all that he has, and he will surely curse You to Your face!" (1:9-11).

It is obvious that God had greatly blessed Job, and God's order is always blessing before discipline. Satan never seeks out the loser. He goes after the person with a reputation, position and possessions. He searches for the men or women who have made their love for God work for them. He hates anyone who loves God. He wants anything that is God's possession.

Satan came against Job during a season of festivities. In the midst of joy he brought sorrow. At a time when Job had many possessions, he was inflicted with poverty. Satan came forcefully with trials at the least expected moment, and he used blitzkrieg tactics. He still does! Satan poured tragedy upon tragedy in Job's life in rapid succession. Before Job had a chance to comprehend one message of doom, another messenger of destruction arrived. Job was not even given time to pray through to victory.

Many pastors have reported to me that they have spent all their energies this past year putting out one fire after another. They are hardly finished with one emergency when another arises. These repeated attacks are satanic tactics. The enemy wants to keep the pressure on until we collapse, blaming ourselves for the failures. It is difficult to come out of a season of prosperity and growth and go into church splits and a loss of key persons through sickness, death or any number of reasons.

But just as blessing precedes testing, comfort accompanies testing. In the hours before the greatest test the disciples ever faced, the crucifixion, Jesus said, "I will not leave you comfortless: I will come to you" (John 14:18, KJV). The New King James Version says, "I will not leave you orphans." Hard times will come to all of us. Christ has never promised immunity from painful circumstances, but He has pledged His presence in the midst of them.

All God's dealings are for our maturing and His self-revelation. Whether those actions seem positive or negative is unimportant. Both blessing and chastisement work for our good, for "we know that all things work together for good to those who love God, to those who are the called according to His purpose" (Romans 8:28). This is easier to embrace when God is enlarging us than when He is reducing us, as Job learned.

Children do not mature without protectors, teachers and role models, and neither do Christians. God does not thrust or drive us into trials. He leads us into them for a learning experience, and He walks with us through them as protector and guide. David knew this promise, for he wrote in his shepherd psalm:

> Yea, though I walk through the valley of the
>   shadow of death,
> I will fear no evil;
> For You are with me;
> Your rod and Your staff, they comfort me
>   (Psalm 23:4).

Life holds its shadows of terror and specters of fear, but the Lord holds our hands as we walk past them.

There is a thesis in the book of Job that Christians often overlook. Jehovah initiated the whole scenario. It was God who challenged Satan with "Have you considered My servant Job, that there is none like him on the earth, a blameless and upright man, one who fears God and shuns evil?" (1:8).

Back to School

Master strategist that He is, God positioned Satan to become an unwitting tool for accomplishing a divine purpose. While attempting to destroy Job's faith, Satan merely succeeded in returning this upright man to the classrooms of life for a special course in theology. This was not a refresher course. God purposed to teach Job things he had never before suspected. Job's knowledge of God was incomplete and narrow. God was in the process of making Job a graduate from grammar school.

Besides facing an entirely new curriculum, Job encountered a new teaching method. I remember the trauma of moving from the eighth grade, where I had a single classroom and the same teacher all day, to the high-school format of changing classrooms and teachers every hour. In time I grew comfortable with the new layout. When I went on to college, where class attendance was not mandatory and much of the learning came through personal research, I faced still another teaching method. I empathize with Job. It is difficult enough to learn new subjects without also having to adjust to new methods of teaching.

Satan pressured Job into high school, but he was not the teacher. He was but the truant officer. In a few quick assaults Satan, here an instrument of God, reversed Job's situation in life. First, all his children were slain. Then his possessions were stolen and destroyed. At this point Job was able to look to the Lord saying,

> The Lord gave, and the Lord has taken away;
> Blessed be the name of the Lord (1:21).

About this time God gave Satan permission to inflict Job physically. He was in dire physical pain, and his appearance was marred with open boils. Those who once revered him now held him in derision. He lost his honored position in the community. Job was so completely reduced to a molten mass that he — or maybe his wife — sent for his out-of-town friends to come. When his friends

24

arrived, they were speechless. Astounded, they sat in silence for seven days.

God Has Comforters Available

For seven days these friends sat silently with him on the heap of ashes, bringing Job the loving comfort he needed desperately. Even in their silence these men related to Job as friend-to-friend. They were trying to feel some of what he felt before sharing their wisdom with him.

At one time a pastor with whom I had ministered repeatedly said, "Iverna, if you ever get into trouble, call me. I'll fly to you, and we'll just sit together and hurt. Even if you are guilty of something, you and I will sit together until we can reach restoration." Such an offer of friendship overwhelmed me. This is the initial picture in the book of Job. These friends did not come to preach to Job. They came because he was in trouble, and they wanted to console him. They came with innocent hearts and pure motives. They came in sympathy and identified in empathy.

At this point of critical suffering Job didn't need platitudes preached from high towers. He needed an understanding love shared at the level of his pain. He needed heart-to-heart communication. He could listen better to someone who had sat where he sat. His friends came to communicate love to Job. They identified physically and emotionally with their friend.

This upright man who had been a teacher of others found himself a student searching for consolation and truth. Job had spent years sitting in the gate of the city as a wise counselor of others. Now he sat on a heap of ashes listening to the silence in the company of his friends. In a rapid sequence of events his comfortable life turned upside down, devastating him. And God scored, orchestrated and conducted it all.

For What Purpose?

This is the heart of the book of Job: God is perfecting in Job what He had declared to Satan was the nature of Job. God called Job "My servant," "a blameless and upright man" and "one who fears God" (1:8). Let's look at the other views of Job presented in the early chapters of his biblical biography. Satan saw Job as an acquisitive man who served God for what he could get. His wife told him to "curse God and die!" (2:9). It seems she saw him as a loser who might just as well renounce his faith since it wasn't working; or she loved him too much to watch him suffer, wasn't mature enough to live through it with him and so suggested he do anything to end the ordeal. The community saw its senior statesman, who sat at the gate as a sort of justice of the peace, as a fallen leader. The greatest man of the East had been reduced to an ash heap.

But God, who sees the end from the beginning, can complete every work He initiates. He declared Job righteous, and He would bring that reality to pass. Paul discovered this. He wrote: "He who has begun a good work in you will complete it until the day of Jesus Christ" (Philippians 1:6).

Between God's proclamation and His product lies His process. And once we grasp God's proclamation, we are qualified to embrace His process to bring it to pass. Most of us delight in the proclamation and look forward to demonstrating the product, but few of us enjoy the divine process. Dianne MacIntosh, who heads the TLC counseling ministry, is gifted with prophetic insight. It is not unusual for her to walk from behind her desk to lay hands on the counselee and pray a prayer that is a direct line from heaven to the heart of the troubled one. It is always a delight to see the change of countenance such a prophetic prayer brings. God speaks to the individual in words of acceptance, hope and assurance.

Unfortunately, some persons accept the spoken word as a specific work; once a word is spoken, it is a living fact. While this may sometimes be true, it is far more frequent for God's inspired word, whether declared, prayed, written or given in counsel, to be a declaration of what can be — far more than what it now is.

If God declares that He sees us as pure and holy, then there is an incumbent responsibility to enter into that purity and holiness. There will be a putting off of some things and a putting on of others. God's change of perspective induces a change of performance.

Just as the architect sees a completed building in his drawings, God sees what we can become by His grace. Between the plans and the dedication of the building lies a season of construction. God reveals His plans for our lives, but there is a time-consuming process before they are complete. By declaring the end from the beginning, God encourages us to participate in the process of change. The pain of construction is made bearable by looking again and again at the "to-scale" model God puts on display.

Quite often the process God uses seems to produce the exact opposite of His proclamation. But just as the impurities must be removed in the refining of metal, so must God deal with the dross in our lives to refine us to a purer standard. It may require the furnace; it often involves much stirring and then a skimming off of the surface of our lives. It is neither instantaneous nor vicarious. It is the divine at work in the person God is purifying for His glory.

When a visitor watched a smelter refining silver in an open pot, he was impressed with how often the refiner stirred and then skimmed the molten silver.

"How does the smelter know when he has pure silver?" he asked.

"When the refiner can see his face mirrored in the metal without distortion" was the reply.

When Jesus can see His image reflected in us without distortion, He stops the process and displays His pure product to others. He knows what He is after, and He will neither rush the process nor stop it until He has achieved His original purpose.

Many wounded and hurting Christians would be on their way to health if they could accept that their lives are in the control of God. Difficult circumstances of suffering can be put behind us when faith can appropriate: "All things work together for good to those who love God, to those who are the called according to His purpose" (Romans 8:28). Often an inspired word from God can tip the balance from exasperation to expectation.

In the book of Job God was not a playwright absent from the set when the scene was played out. He was with Job in every step of this experience. Job longed to find a God who was not lost. "He Himself has said, 'I will never leave you nor forsake you' " (Hebrews 13:5). God was not absent. He merely presented Himself through human channels. Job yearned for a chance to "come to His seat," while all the time God sat with him on the ashes.

God had set the limiting boundaries for Satan's actions, and He sent comforters who would eventually teach Job things about God that he had not yet learned. God's communication with Job at the end of the book shows that He heard every word spoken by these five men. He had been present all the time. In the schoolroom of life He was the subject and the Teacher. Eliphaz, Bildad, Zophar and Elihu would be instruments through whom God communicated.

Job the Complainer

It was Job himself who broke the seven-day silence of his friends by cursing the day of his birth (3:1).

"Why did I not die at birth? Why did I not perish when I came from the womb?" he cried (3:11). Obviously Job was in deep depression. Except for his fear of God, he would have taken his wife's advice to "curse God and die."

James spoke of "the patience of Job" (James 5:11, KJV), leading us to visualize a calm, collected, aged gentleman swaying in his rocking chair on the front porch amidst all his troubles. We need to remind ourselves that the word *patience* once meant "perseverance." More modern translations, including the New King James Version, use the word *perseverance*. Job did persevere, but he did not do so patiently, as we now use the word. He persevered with mighty protestations.

Job complained bitterly. He wished he had never been born. He wanted to die. He wanted out of his classroom before the lessons began. Like Elijah, he could do well in time of victory, but he wanted to die when adversity came. He successfully counseled others in trouble, but he could not apply that counsel to himself when the pressure came.

He cried:

> The thing I greatly feared has come upon me,
> And what I dreaded has happened to me
>   (3:25).

It is not likely he had lived his comfortable life in fear and dread of the calamities that had now come upon him, although many fail to enjoy today's blessings for fear they may soon be taken away. This is called anxiety and is forbidden to the Christian, who is told to take no thought for tomorrow. What had happened to him was so unusual it was impossible to anticipate. More likely, he was referring to the swiftness with which these events came. Before he could handle the impact of one tragedy, another swooped down upon him. When he heard of one misfortune, he naturally dreaded another, and, sure enough, it came.

The sympathetic comforters had already been so overwhelmed at the sight of Job that they sat in silence. Job now stirs them further by revealing his innermost thoughts. They hear no immediate expression of faith or trust in God. There is no blessing of God for past favors. There is not even a thanksgiving that God had spared his life. The picture of Job at this point must be painted in dark hues against a black background.

Job didn't seem to react so much to the adversity, loss and pain as he did to the deep-seated question why. His situation violated his very concept of God, his doctrine of righteousness and prosperity. He seemed to handle the physical loss far better than the loss of his basic tenets of faith.

When God granted Satan permission to withdraw the very things Job used as measurements of divine approval, Job was deeply disturbed. He questioned the whole system of faith he had developed in his years of walking with God. What had happened to him did not fit his theological concepts.

Job is not unique in this problem. In the upper room, right after serving the last supper,

> The Lord said, "Simon, Simon! Indeed, Satan has asked for you, that he may sift you as

wheat. But I have prayed for you, that your faith should not fail; and when you have returned to Me, strengthen your brethren" (Luke 22:31-32).

Peter's code of faith was to undergo a severe testing, but Christ, the intercessor, had prayed to the Father that the true faith would not fail but be strengthened.

God's goal for Job was an enlargement of his concepts of God. As David later testified, "Thou hast enlarged me when I was in distress" (Psalm 4:1, KJV). Growth is painful, but it is profitable. Faith may be shaken, but it does not shatter. The very things that come to destroy our faith can establish and enlarge it.

The enemy may remove "things," but he cannot separate us from true faith in God. As Paul wrote,

For I am persuaded that neither death nor life, nor angels nor principalities nor powers, nor things present nor things to come, nor height nor depth, nor any other created thing, shall be able to separate us from the love of God which is in Christ Jesus our Lord (Romans 8:38-39).

THREE

Recognizing the Living Word in Prophecy

The book of Job is not about a man whom God turned over to Satan to see how much he could suffer and still not deny God. The Lord takes no pleasure in determining our breaking point. He knows quite well where it is. The book of Job is about God's seeking to reveal Himself to us. And God tempers all His actions toward us with grace. It might be worth noting that Job's story has five steps, and five is the number of grace.

(1) Job was challenged by Satan.

(2) He was tested by God.

(3) He was questioned by his friends.

(4) He was restored by revelation.

(5) He was rewarded by grace.

It is probable that everything in the life of believers falls into these five steps. Until we have experienced this progressive work of grace, we will not know God experientially. How can we really know that Jehovah is a healer until we've been sick and He heals us? We may know it intellectually, but we don't know it factually until we have experienced it.

This is what was going on in the life of Job. He was

being brought into an experiential knowledge of God that would replace his theoretical concepts. If we glimpse ahead to the end of the story, we can see the results of God's work. Job told God:

> I have heard of You by the hearing of the ear,
> But now my eye sees You (42:5).

God purposes that all satanic challenges to our lives will cause us to see the Lord. During these times of testings God mercifully provides further revelation about Himself through the prophetic channel.

In this and following chapters we will walk through the last three steps of Job's story, gleaning from it lessons for hearing God's word today.

Eliphaz as Instructor

Eliphaz was most likely the highest-ranking friend, being the oldest of these wise men. He spoke first, visualizing himself as a comforter, though God sent him as an instructor. How often we are tools of God without knowing it; we speak without realizing the flow of divine inspiration. I never cease to be amazed at the number of persons who tell me that God spoke through me, giving them specific directions for their lives or great encouragement in the midst of personal tribulation. When I reflect on our time together, I remember only table conversation, but they recall prophetic truth. I shared what I felt at the moment, but they heard the voice of God in that communication. Since I was but the channel, not the source, of the communication, I didn't share their awareness of God's involvement.

It is likely that Job's comforters were equally unaware

of being mouthpieces for God. They taught what they had received from God, their source. "Such as I have give I thee" (Acts 3:6, KJV) was a working principle long before Peter declared it to the lame man at Gate Beautiful. A modern equivalent of "we have this treasure in earthen vessels" (2 Corinthians 4:7) might be "our treasure is in handy dispensers." Over the years God had put divine wisdom in these men. Now Job was given an opportunity to draw some of it out for personal use.

Eliphaz initially showed great courtesy to Job. He started by asking permission to speak with Job (4:2) and then chatted about better days in Job's life. He reminded Job of being an instructor of many (4:3) and of having strengthened the weak (4:3-5). He discussed Job's reverence and the integrity that long had been his hope (4:6). Eliphaz's modest and complimentary style should have opened Job to receive instruction.

When none of this produced a spark of hope in Job, Eliphaz used a nearly standard religious ploy. He brought up a moving, personal religious experience to give greater authority to what he was saying. He recalled a vision in the night — so frightening as to make his hair stand up (4:15). The person or angel in the vision (Eliphaz admitted he could not make out the form of the creature) had spoken of the righteousness of God: No mortal can be more righteous than God; even the imputed righteousness of the angels of heaven is incomparable to the righteousness of almighty God.

Eliphaz encouraged Job to appeal to God (5:8) and gently challenged him not to despise God's discipline:

> Behold, happy is the man whom God corrects;
> Therefore do not despise the chastening of the Almighty.

> For He bruises, but He binds up;
> He wounds, but His hands make whole
>   (5:17-18).

He correctly put Job in the hands of the Almighty —
not the devil.

In his third speech Eliphaz prophesied profuse praise
about God, encouraging Job to realize that God would be
his treasure (22:25) and his delight (22:26) and that He
would answer Job's prayers (22:27). This friend spoke of
a pure God who purposed restoration for Job:

> If you return to the Almighty, you will be
>   built up....
> Yes, the Almighty will be your gold
> And your precious silver;
> For then you will have your delight in the Al-
>   mighty,
> And lift up your face to God.
> You will make your prayer to Him,
> He will hear you,
> And you will pay your vows (22:23, 25-27).

He affirmed that Job would again have a prophetic
flow (22:28) and that exaltation would come (22:29).

Eliphaz emphasized the *purity* of God in all three
speeches. What he said was beautiful, genuine and true.
He painted a picture of God that is reiterated in the New
Testament. By his own testimony this view of God came
to Job through a heavenly messenger. But Job didn't hear
the message. Eventually we'll discuss the inadequacies
of Job that kept his ears plugged. First let's look at the
problems with Eliphaz's delivery. What I've detailed
above — a brief summary of Eliphaz's word from the
Lord — is only half the story.

Projection of Guilt Veils Divine Revelation

Eliphaz may have received a supernatural revelation of God, but he dared to intrude his personal opinion of Job on that vision. To his mind, the contrast between a pure God and a ruined Job could only mean that Job had sinned. In an apparent effort to move Job to repentance, Eliphaz expounded the doctrine of the absolute and horrible fate of the wicked — including the prosperous, implying that Job was in this category.

There can be no doubt that Eliphaz judged Job guilty of some sin that had prompted this severe punishment. He even gave a detailed list of the kinds of sin he assumed Job had committed (22:6-11). Since the only rational answer to Job's predicament seemed to be sin, Eliphaz intertwined his personal conclusions with his divine revelation.

Eliphaz had paid the price to get a revelation of God. He journeyed a distance and sat long and sympathetically with his friend. Instead of merely sharing what God had given him to share, he mixed his deductions, based on human observation, with his revelation and created such a bitter mixture of truth and error that Job would not drink it.

Job knew the projected condemnation was false. He was well aware of the standard of righteousness by which he had lived. He believed in the integrity of his heart, and he knew he was innocent of the crimes on Eliphaz's indictment list. Job logically reasoned that if the message was from God, it would all be true. When he saw untruth in it, he considered the entire message false.

At this stage in Job's spiritual maturity his relationship with God rested on personal integrity. As he saw it, if he lost his integrity, he would be cut off from God. This line of thinking made Job get defensive. Correctly, he refused to accept a wrong concept about himself. Incorrectly, he also rejected a true concept about God.

In maintaining his defensive position, Job blocked out everything God had said through Eliphaz. What Eliphaz said would have greatly enlarged Job's appreciation of God, but he heard the words only in his head. His heart could not grasp this revelation. A wounded spirit is seldom teachable.

Eliphaz gave Job advice based on "if I were in your shoes...." I hate it when people say that to me. I want to put them in my shoes — or put my shoes on them — forcefully.

Prophetic Pollution Demands Purification

Eliphaz was guilty of polluting a message from God. He was neither the first nor the last to do so.

Impure prophecy has polluted almost every move of God. Some who operate in this gift or calling become wide open to the spirit world but are too immature in the ways of God to know what spirit is operating. They become almost clairvoyant and feel that they have answers for everyone. They dare to break up marriages, command people to sell their houses and give the money to prophets. They prophesy pastors out of their churches and move people from one geographic location to another. They do this in the name of God, but it is unlikely the Spirit of the Lord is involved.

Some people will respond favorably to anything that begins with "Thus says the Lord" — especially if the person speaking is well-known and accepted. We need to be mature enough to realize that the devil is not interested in speaking through just anyone. It is those who have divine credibility in the body of Christ that the enemy seeks to pollute. I am fearfully aware of how desperately

Satan would like to add a bit of mixture into what I preach. Those who have watched my life and whose lives my ministry has blessed tend to accept everything I say as a "word from God."

God knows my heart better than anyone else, even better than I do. He knows that I want to give only the perfect, pure word of God. However, I must remind myself constantly that all of God's messages come through imperfect channels. As Paul put it, "But we have this treasure in earthen vessels, that the excellence of the power may be of God and not of us" (2 Corinthians 4:7). This treasure of God's spoken word comes in clay pots. The pots need to be purified lest they flavor the contents.

When God called Isaiah to the prophetic office, He first purged his mouth with a burning coal from the golden altar of incense of heaven. God's prophets still need their mouths purged before speaking in the name of God. The coal for that purging comes from the place of prayer and praise. If that altar is not approached regularly, there will be no purging of the mouth.

I am frightened of people who study what is happening in a service and then give prophecy that is based upon their observations. They are behaving just like Job's comforters. Suppose someone sees you weeping. They approach you and say, "The Lord has just spoken to me about you. I don't know a thing about you, but you are sad." That wasn't God. Any perceptive person could have deduced the same thing. But then things get complicated. Because that one statement was true, whatever else is said is often accepted as truth from God.

The comforters of Job were not liars. Everything Eliphaz said about God was true. Unfortunately his message contained a mixture. His deductions were based upon a seven-day observance of Job. While picturing a sovereign God, he so contrasted Job with God as to condemn Job as a sinner. His sermon was fine. His altar call was colored and prejudiced. He understood the facts correctly but drew wrong conclusions based on those facts. His counsel or prophetic insight was a mixture of right and wrong, of God and man.

God sends teachers to instruct us in the ways of the Lord, but He wants the messengers to be cautious in the way they make the "altar call." We must remember that even truth improperly applied becomes effective error.

The Message, Not the Messenger, Is Authoritative

We know that Christ gave gifts to persons and gave gifted persons to the church. Paul wrote, "And He Himself gave some to be apostles, some prophets, some evangelists, and some pastors and teachers" (Ephesians 4:11). For several years now there has been a fresh emphasis upon these fivefold ministry gifts, but in our search to recognize God's gifts among us we have often given too high an honor to the people who fill these offices. Just as an apostle is not a dictator, he is also not a judge. He or she is but a communicator. Words have no more authority than the one who spoke the words. If the prophet speaks the words that God gave, then the authority of God is in the message. If the words are from the speaker's mind and heart, they carry no more weight than the words of any other person. It is not the office or the gift that gives strength to the message. It is the authority behind that gift that empowers certain messages.

When I was in grammar school my parents pastored in North Bend, Oregon. The parsonage stood on such a steep hillside that when my brothers wanted to play baseball, they had to go up the hill about a block to a level piece of ground. When Mother put the evening meal on the table, she expected the entire family to be present. She would give a five-minute warning that needed to be heeded; if you missed the prayer over the meal, you missed the meal.

On one occasion she sent me to the ball field to tell the boys to come to dinner. Climbing the hill to the play-ground, I called as loudly as my youthful voice could cry, "Dinner's ready!"

It was an exciting game, and the boys chose to ignore me.

"Come on," I shouted. "It's time to eat."

"Go on home," they said.

I cried all the way home. "What's wrong, honey?" Mother asked as I walked into the house.

"The boys won't come home," I responded.

"You go back and say, '*Mother said* come to dinner!'"

My legs ached as I climbed the hill again. I stomped my little feet and shouted, "Mother said...."

That's all it took. My brothers stopped the game im-mediately, and we rushed back to the house to wash for dinner.

My message became authoritative when the boys rec-ognized I was not speaking of myself. Mother's authority had to be respected, or they would not get supper.

This authority of command is so important that Jesus told His disciples that even the Holy Spirit "will not speak on His own authority, but whatever He hears He will speak; and He will tell you things to come. He will glorify Me, for He will take of what is Mine and declare it to you" (John 16:13-14). If the Holy Spirit speaks only the words of the Father and the Son, we need to be careful that we relay in God's name nothing but His very words.

Inspiration or Interpretation?

Perhaps the greatest error made by Job's friends was in seeking to reveal Job to himself instead of revealing

Jehovah to Job. Our great need is not introspection but extrospection. The inward look will discourage and perhaps destroy us, but the upward look will encourage us and bring us life. Job's friends described God accurately, but they caused Job to look at himself instead of at God, whom they had unveiled in the spirit of prophecy.

This failure of Job's comforters underscores the fact that when a prophet seeks to interpret a prophecy, the message is often missed entirely. A pastor friend of mine who flows in a mature level of prophecy tells of a visit by a well-known minister from another country. He declared from the pulpit: "The Lord has sent me with a message for this church." What followed was a serious condemnation of the pastor, ending in a call for his immediate repentance so that God would remove a curse from his life. This astounded the pastor and greatly confused the congregation.

That afternoon the pastor went to the hotel room of this minister and pointed out the impropriety of what he had done. He asked where he was coming from. The brother said he had sensed a coldness in the church during the service and felt that hidden sin was restricting the flow of God's presence.

"Why didn't you say that?" the pastor asked.

"Well, I assumed that you were the problem, and I wanted to deal with it at its source."

The prophet replaced a message that might have been redemptive to the congregation with his personal interpretation. This produced such confusion among the people that they began to rise against their "unrepentant pastor," who was not guilty of wrongdoing. Later events did reveal there was sin in the congregation, but not among the leadership. That was a presumption by the guest, but when he spoke it as a word from God, it became a tool of the enemy.

The words God sent to comfort Job became the source of his greatest torment because the speakers misapplied the message. Had Job been mature enough spiritually, he could have received the prophetic word in spite of the prophet or his application. Unfortunately, Job rejected the revelation of God because the application the prophets made declared Job to be guilty when he knew he was innocent. God desires that we learn to recognize the living Word in prophecy in spite of the channel through which it may come.

Judging Prophecy

It would be easy to put the full responsibility for purity of communication upon the prophets. Few, if any, of us want to accept personal responsibility for our spiritual walk. While Scripture does hold the prophet responsible for what he or she speaks in God's name, it holds the believers equally responsible for what they hear and attribute to God. Regarding the gift of prophecy Paul wrote:

> Let two or three prophets speak, and let the others judge. But if anything is revealed to another who sits by, let the first keep silent. For you can all prophesy one by one, that all may learn and all may be encouraged. And the spirits of the prophets are subject to the prophets. For God is not the author of confusion but of peace, as in all the churches of the saints (1 Corinthians 14:29-33).

In these verses the Holy Spirit teaches us seven things about the operation of the gift of prophecy.

(1) It should be done in small doses — "two or three."

42

(2) It should then be judged.

(3) No one should monopolize the operation of this gift.

(4) Where the spirit of prophecy is present, all may prophesy.

(5) The Holy Spirit never makes a robot of the channel. The spirit of the person prophesying is always in control.

(6) If the prophetic words produce confusion, be assured God is not at fault.

(7) God is the author of peace, and the purpose of His communication is to bring us to peace with Himself.

John the apostle gives an eighth criterion for prophecy: "Worship God! For the testimony of Jesus is the spirit of prophecy" (Revelation 19:10). A critical basis for judging the purity of a prophetic utterance is whether it gives testimony to Jesus.

Judging a prophecy will demand an enlarged knowledge of God. This was a weakness in the life of Job. He had a very limited knowledge of God. For instance, after his children had a season of celebration, Job offered sacrifices to make propitiation for any sin they may have committed (1:5). Job lived in the same spiritual insecurity many religious people have embraced. They envision a God who is looking for something wrong for which He can punish them. They know little or nothing about a God of love who is calling them into a personal walk with Him. They have so embraced the law of God that they have not discovered His grace.

We need to be charitable toward Job, realizing he lacked our biblical revelation of God. Job was among the early pioneers in receiving the revelation of God that Adam lost through sin. He lacked the guidelines and religious heritage that have formed our understanding.

We also need to realize that Job was excluded from the

heavenly conversation between God and Satan, which is recorded in Job 1-2. He did not know what God thought of him or that God had thrown him in the face of Satan as a challenge. I think Job would have responded differently if he had known what we know now.

Paul realized that we do not always have sufficient facts available to make proper judgments. He wrote:

> But with me it is a very small thing that I should be judged by you or by a human court. In fact, I do not even judge myself. For I know nothing against myself, yet I am not justified by this; but He who judges me is the Lord. Therefore judge nothing before the time, until the Lord comes, who will both bring to light the hidden things of darkness and reveal the counsels of the hearts; and then each one's praise will come from God (1 Corinthians 4:3-5).

Paul knew that God alone fully understands the heart's inner motivations and Satan's outer hindrances; Paul would wait until all the facts were in before accepting condemnation. That takes progressive perseverance. But, in Paul's case, it was enlightened persistence, for he knew that God had information He had not yet shared with Paul. Job did not know this.

While there are factors as unknown to us as God's challenge to Satan was unknown to Job, there are many things we do know that Job did not understand. God's Word clearly tells us how God feels about us by calling us the children of God and the objects of His special love.

Prophetic Word or Word of a Prophet?

Even though we may know the prophet or channel of prophecy, it does not excuse us from judging that prophecy. The most trusted friend could speak out of his or her compassion and put God's name on it. Sometimes a person will express a vindictiveness in a prophecy. Unless recognized quickly, this can produce a false sense of condemnation in the listener.

Many modern Christians are afraid to reject anything spoken by one who claims to be a prophet or prophetess. This fear is especially compounded when the person has told about deep spiritual revelations. But stop. Stand on the truth. If someone declares, "God has shown me something about you..." and what he or she declares is not true, don't accept it. Sometimes we simply have to say "baloney!"

The body of Christ needs to mature until we can distinguish a true prophetic word from merely the word of a prophet. There is often a prophetic word in the words of a prophet, but not everything said is true prophecy. Those speaking to Job had great truth in their messages, but they had such a mixture of error that God greatly condemned them and insisted that Job make propitiation for them.

Some years ago my brother was a guest speaker in a prestigious church in Hawaii. While he was reading his text, a person in the balcony stood and prophesied about my brother's ministry and its worldwide acceptance. He also spoke broadly of great pride in my brother's life. He pronounced severe judgment upon him unless he repented immediately and publicly.

Judson ignored the message and began to preach. A man on the main floor stood up and demanded immediate repentance. When Judson said he had nothing to repent of, the man became so incensed he had to be taken out of the service. Within minutes this man had circled the building and found a rear entrance that led to the platform. He ran across the rostrum like a charging marine in an invasion. Grabbing my brother by the shoulders, he forced him to the floor, all the while screaming, "The prophet called for you to repent. Repent!"

It took several ushers to pull the man off Judson. Somehow he regained his composure and returned to his morning message, only to be interrupted again by the "prophet" in the balcony. This time the speaker said Judson's marriage was falling apart because of immorality.

"That's what I have been waiting for," Judson said. "You have finally said something that I can disprove." Calling to his wife in the congregation, Judson said, "Eleanor, please stand up. Is our marriage in jeopardy?"

She denied the "prophet's" accusation and said that the two of them had just enjoyed nearly a month of ministry together in Australia and New Zealand and that it had been like a second honeymoon.

Judson says that what the man said about his worldwide ministry was true, but what he said about sin and immorality was untrue. If he had not been able to discern between what was correct and what was erroneous, he could have responded to the pressure to repent. The congregation would probably have accepted his broken spirit and his ministry may have continued, but the admission would have been false, and the results would have been equally spurious.

We who have the benefit of the Bible know that God is a speaking God who can be understood by people. He may use a variety of ways to communicate, but we can hear His voice. Job needed to learn how to recognize the living Word in prophecy. He failed with the first speaker, but there were more to come. Slowly God was teaching him to refine truth from prophecy.

FOUR

Refining Truth From Prophecy

In northeastern Washington a weekly newspaper, the *Statesman-Examiner*, ran a story about the opening of a zinc mine that "has excellent exploration potential." But keep reading, and the statistics boggle the mind. This is not my area of expertise, but I can't understand the profitability of having to handle a ton of dirt to get less than 150 pounds of ore.

Yet when it comes to prophecy, we Christians tend to demand 100 percent pure ore. Why? Aren't we able to refine divine truth from the mixture in which we generally find it? On extremely rare occasions we read of a person finding a nugget of pure gold, but most gold mined in the world today is mixed in with other minerals, even dirt. It must be refined in the smelter. This is time consuming and costly, but the gold is worth it.

The psalmists compared God's words to highly refined gold. David wrote:

> The fear of the Lord is clean, enduring forever;
> The judgments of the Lord are true and righteous altogether.

> More to be desired are they than gold,
>   Yea, than much fine gold (Psalm 19:9-10).

Another said:

> Therefore I love Your commandments
> More than gold, yes, than fine gold! (Psalm
>   119:127).

Job had to learn that the fine gold of God's words often comes encrusted in rock and soil.

Bildad's Raw Ore

Bildad, the second of Job's friends to speak, lacked the graciousness of Eliphaz. He had heard the first speech of his companion and Job's defense of his innocence, which seemed to confirm Bildad's conviction that Job was guilty of sin. Bildad charged Job with producing nothing but a big wind:

> How long will you speak these things,
> And the words of your mouth be like a
>   strong wind? (8:2).

I have listened to my share of speakers who have come across as bags of wind. Sometimes I wonder if congregations think that about my speaking! The Indians used to say, "Heap big smoke, but no fire!" That's what Bildad said to Job as an introduction. I don't think his approach would win an award at a Dale Carnegie conference on how to win friends and influence people.

The heart of Bildad's speech was the justice of God, and we can well imagine that occasionally Job said a loud amen! Job himself was a great proclaimer of the justice of God. It is woven into many of his addresses. But this golden truth from Bildad's lips was mixed with much rock and soil. By the fourth sentence of his oration Bildad dared say:

> If your sons have sinned against Him,
> He has cast them away for their transgres-
>   sion (8:4).

That hurt. Job, as the priest of his home, had offered sacrifices for his sons and daughters — even for unintentional sins (1:8). Bildad's charge that the children perished because a just God couldn't stand to let such sinners live challenged both Job's training of his family and his faith as a priest.

I assume from this brash statement that Bildad lacked children or felt that his children were living righteously. How easy it is to point an accusing finger when we feel guiltless. The person with a quality marriage can be heartless in looking at a Christian marriage that ended in the divorce court. Those whose children are in the ministry often become accusers of parents whose children fall to drugs, immorality or crime. The crushed don't need condemnation; they need comfort. We need to reread Isaiah's words: " 'Comfort, yes, comfort My people!' says your God" (40:1).

Job's children were dead, and Bildad spoke a "prophetic word" that they had died for their transgressions. Why can't we let God's people die in peace? I frequently hear of Christians who have not been permitted to die in grace or say good-bye to their families because some well-meaning persons have stood by prophesying that they would live.

Projected Desire Is Not Prophecy

Recently a five-year-old boy lay dying of cancer. Someone prophesied a word that the Lord was going to use this sickness to demonstrate the miracle power of God. As a result the leadership urged the entire congregation to fast. For eight days most of the believers in this group fasted and prayed for the complete healing of the child. On the eighth day the boy died.

I arrived two days later to conduct a series of services. You can imagine the emotional temperature of that congregation. Confusion reigned from parents to pastor. There was a blanket of death and defeat over the congregation. Assured that the voice had been the voice of God, the congregation accepted personal blame for failure. Their sense of guilt could not have been much greater if they had actually killed the boy.

My answer to their condition was to preach the lordship of Jesus Christ. I assured them that God is not the author of confusion. If He had declared His plan to heal the boy, there would have been no death. I did not say that the Lord "took" the boy; I simply declared that Jesus Christ is Lord of all situations. He is in control no matter who says what! Just because someone prophesies "thus saith the Lord" does not release us from the responsibility of determining if, indeed, it really is the word of the Lord. Had the congregation refined this message, they would never have put their trust in it.

The book of Job shows that righteous people do suffer at times, but not always because there is sin in their lives. It is true that God is a just God. It is equally true that "the wages of sin is death" (Romans 6:23), but this cannot be reduced to the simplistic equation that all suffering and death are the result of personal sin. This is what Bildad was trying to sell to Job. Fortunately, Job wasn't buying.

Bildad's Veins of Truth

No person or company will expend the energy or money necessary to mine ore from the ground unless it has already been determined that there is a deposit of precious metal in that ore. We could ignore the three speeches of Bildad if they were all rock and clay. We dare not, for buried deep in this mixture is a deposit of truth that should have encouraged Job in his depression.

There are at least four precious gems in the first discourse alone. In spite of the mixture of personal prejudice, the prophetic fire burning in Bildad caused him to say:

> Though your beginning was small,
> Yet your latter end would increase abun-
>   dantly (8:7).

Granted that he mixed in the prerequisite:

> If you were pure and upright,
> Surely now He would awake for you,
> And prosper your rightful habitation (8:6).

But this should not have disturbed Job too deeply, for the backbone of everything he said was that Job really was pure and upright. Furthermore, these are the first words God spoke concerning Job.

How beautifully did the prophet echo the words God had spoken to Satan regarding Job. God was offering Job an insight into the divine heart. Not only were the prophet's ears tuned to what God said, but his eyes were open to what God was about to do in restoring Job to a greater prosperity than he possessed when Satan began stripping him. These words were more precious than gold, but they had to be refined to be seen (heard) for what they were.

The second vein of rich mineral found in Bildad's communication is: "Behold, God will not cast away the blameless" (8:20). We could easily miss this nugget, for it is buried in Bildad's projection of guilt. Even if you have to go through a ton of ore to get a hundred pounds of metal, it is worth it. God had already declared Job blameless. Job had claimed to be blameless. This, then, was prophetic assurance that, in spite of the current testing and trial, Job was not being cast away from God's presence. Hallelujah!

In times of pressure we may *feel* as if God has cast us off, but our feelings do not consistently reflect the facts. Sometimes I am very conscious of the presence of God; other times I have no sense of that presence at all. But He is there. It is always amazing to me to see the results at the end of a service when I have ministered in pure faith with no feeling of the divine intervention. My emotional and physical exhaustion have numbed my senses but not hindered God from flowing through me as a vessel.

As Job continued to listen, he could have heard God speak to him through harsh Bildad when he said:

> He will yet fill your mouth with laughing,
> And your lips with rejoicing (8:21).

The marginal reading is: "Your lips with shouts of joy." On the ash heap Job had nothing for which to be joyful. He had lost every joy-producing thing in his life. God sent a message to his servant saying:

> Weeping may endure for a night,
> But joy comes in the morning (Psalm 30:5).

The fourth rich vein of truth buried in Bildad's words was:

> Those who hate you will be clothed with
>   shame,
> And the dwelling place of the wicked will
>   come to nothing (8:22).

No matter what tone of voice Bildad may have used in giving this, no one can dispute that this was the word of the Lord, for Jesus said virtually the same thing. In the synagogue in Nazareth one Sabbath, the priests invited Jesus to address the assembled Jews. Asking for the Isaiah writing, division number 2, He unrolled the leather scroll until He found the passage that read:

> The Spirit of the Lord God is upon Me...
> To proclaim the acceptable year of the Lord,
> And the day of vengeance of our God;
> To comfort all who mourn (Isaiah 61:1-2).

Jesus coupled divine vengeance with human comfort. Here Bildad does the same thing.

David understood the importance of God's intervention against his enemies. He wrote:

> The righteous shall rejoice when he sees the
>   vengeance;
> He shall wash his feet in the blood of the
>   wicked (Psalm 58:10).

It should have comforted Job to know that others would not always trample on him. God sent him word that heavenly vengeance would be poured out on Job's adversaries. It is proper for God to chasten His children, but

He deals severely with those who jump in to help Him. That is the theme of the book of Amos.

Bildad's Slag Pile

It is impossible to get to the mineral-bearing ore without blasting and hauling away tons of useless rock, which the miners dump in piles, forming small mountains at the mouth of the mine. They call them slag piles.

The second speech of Bildad was true slag. He was harsh in his attitude toward Job and dared to ask him if he expected the world to stop for him (18:4). The rest of the discourse dwells on the horrible fate of the wicked, and he slants it to picture Job. It builds a formidable mound of coarse gravel, from which no amount of refining could extract valuable metal.

Job's response to this tirade shows that he didn't know how to handle it. He didn't realize it was rocks and dirt that needed to be cast aside. Job's answer ended with:

> Now if it is not so, who will prove me a liar,
> And make my speech worth nothing?
> (24:25).

Out of patience with Bildad, Job is getting very defensive.

> Then Bildad the Shuhite answered and said:
>   "Dominion and fear belong to Him;
> He makes peace in His high places.
> Is there any number to His armies?
> Upon whom does His light not rise?
> How then can man be righteous before God?
> Or how can he be pure who is born of a
>   woman?

54

If even the moon does not shine,
And the stars are not pure in His sight,
How much less man, who is a maggot,
And a son of man, who is a worm?" (25:1-6).

What wonderful truth flows in this pageant of praise that formed Bildad's third and final lecture. Bildad declared that dominion and authority belong to God. This man of wisdom refused to see Satan as having authority in the lives of the righteous. He declared that Jehovah held government in His hands and was exclusively worthy of our fear, adoration and worship.

Bildad felt that, in his arguments, Job tried to show himself as God's equal. He wanted Job to recognize the distance between himself and his Creator. He sought to get Job's eyes off himself and onto his God. This is a valid use of the prophetic gift (Revelation 19:10). He recognized that peace must have its source in the Prince of Peace and that there is no measurement of God's power. What comfort this should have been to Job, but it is difficult to accept comfort from a man who has falsely accused you of sin. How can we recognize nuggets of gold when we have just had to deal with truckloads of worthless rock?

At one time or another we have all found ourselves in a circumstance similar to Job's. With a desperate need for a comforting word from God, we have received such a mixture of criticism, guilt projection and condemnation that we have wondered if the message flowed from a gift of prophecy or a gift of suspicion. Even if there had been a comforting word from God, we could not have heard it, because we had not learned to refine a prophetic word to separate the silver from the slag.

The Refining Process

When Paul wrote, "However, the spiritual is not first, but the natural, and afterward the spiritual" (1 Corinthians 15:46), he expressed a principle of interpretation. The things in our natural realm are illustrative of things in the spiritual realm. It should follow, then, that the way we refine ore to get pure metal in our earthly smelters illustrates how we can refine truth from "mixture" in prophecy. Smelting involves four fundamental steps: crushing, melting, purifying and molding.

Once the ore arrives at the smelter, the rock is crushed into small particles. You can likewise work to reduce a prophetic word to small particles. Take it apart. If the prophecy has been tape recorded, transcribe it and go over it repeatedly. If it was not recorded, write down what you can remember. The sooner, the better! Study it. What is obviously true? Just as important, what is obviously false? What portions could be true or false, but you are not quite certain? Does any of it violate the clear teaching of Scripture?

After the rock is crushed, it is put in a crucible and taken to a superheated furnace. After dissecting a mixed prophecy into the smallest possible segments, pour it into the crucible of prayer and take it to the fire. Don't bother with the fire of anxiety or desire. Smelting takes an abnormally hot fire. The Bible tells us, "For our God is a consuming fire" (Hebrews 12:29). Let the heat of God's presence melt the metal trapped in the rock.

As the crushed ore is heated, the unwanted metals melt first, and the refiner pours or siphons them off. As the temperature of the furnace increases, the next level of mineral melts and is drawn off the surface of the crucible. Finally the crucible reaches the temperature necessary to release the silver or gold. As it melts, it is no longer mixed with other elements.

God knows the temperature needed to release truth from error. He will repeatedly heat your heart until He has removed every trace of the false — but this takes time. Refining cannot be done in a microwave oven.

Finally the desired metal is poured into molds, forming usable ingots. God desires to pour the refined truth of prophecy into our hearts, making it available for whatever use the Holy Spirit may desire. Refining truth is of little account if it isn't applied to daily living. Prophecy in a notebook may form great memories, but God is in the business of building character in our lives.

It appears that Job did not know how to respond to a prophet's rebuke and still embrace prophetic truth. He certainly is not the last believer with this problem.

FIVE

REBUKING IN PROPHECY

W hat we do not know about Job's comforters far exceeds what we do know. Peloubet's Bible Dictionary says:

> Eliphaz [came] from Teman south of the Dead Sea, 200 miles from Uz. Bildad, [came] from Shuah near the Euphrates, a sage, of literary culture, quoting proverbs and traditions of the fathers. Zophar [came] from Naamah sixty miles south of the Dead Sea. The ordinary good man of the day, uttering common thoughts in a common way, sometimes sharp and bigoted.

If the research of these editors is accurate, these friends paid a great price to come to the afflicted Job. Eliphaz's two-hundred-mile trek, probably by camel, was a major sacrifice. But even Zophar's trip of sixty miles was adventurous in his day. These men did not travel this far to condemn Job. They came to comfort their friend.

Each man offered great truths about God, for we can sustain their theology with comparative passages found elsewhere in the Bible.

Zophar was concerned with the wisdom of God. Most of his first speech is a contrast between God's wisdom and man's limited knowledge. This divine wisdom is a strong New Testament theme. Paul taught that the wisdom of this world was transient and ineffective. He saw divine wisdom resident in Jesus, referring to "Christ the power of God and the wisdom of God" (1 Corinthians 1:24) and "the Father and of Christ in whom are hidden all the treasures of wisdom and knowledge" (Colossians 2:2-3). He taught that this wisdom could flow as one of the gifts of the Spirit (1 Corinthians 12:8), and he called the indwelling Spirit "the spirit of wisdom" (Ephesians 1:17).

It is proper, then, that Zophar should speak to Job about the wisdom of God. God sent these messages to Job to comfort and sustain him during his great test. We have observed, however, that although the messages concerning God were true, the applications the speakers made of these messages were false.

Job's friends were caught in the trap of trying to know God's why. They saw Job's condition in the light of cause and effect. The contrast between a holy, righteous, just and wise God and a person as devastated as Job was more than the men could rationalize. In their eyes only serious sin could cause God to deal so severely with His servants — so they continued to probe for sin in Job's life.

Knowing he had not sinned, Job refused their guilt projection. This increased the perplexity of Eliphaz, Bildad, Zophar and Elihu, who remained convinced there could be no other reason for Job's condition except God's punishment for sin; each speaker became more outspoken against Job.

When Zophar got his turn to speak, he was furious with

Job for insisting he was blameless. Zophar suggested that Job was helplessly stupid, not wise:

> For an empty-headed man will be wise,
> When a wild donkey's colt is born a man
> (11:12).

(This points to Job!)
From there on Zophar's words to Job became even more harsh and rebuking.

Rebuking in Prophecy
May Reflect Wrong Concepts of God

Zophar rebuked Job out of deep concern, not lack of concern. Note the introduction to his first speech:

> When you mock, should no one rebuke you?
> For you have said,
> "My doctrine is pure,
> And I am clean in your eyes" (11:3-4).

Job's claims of innocence incited Zophar to call for Job's immediate repentance. When this was not forthcoming, Zophar heaped judgment after judgment upon Job. Zophar's entire second speech, Job 20, is a list of God's condemnation and punishment of the righteous hypocrite. You can bet these comforters fixed their gaze on Job as Zophar taught this exciting truth of divine revelation. Zophar was absolutely certain that unrighteous behavior was the only rational explanation for Job's predicament.

Zophar had his reasons for rebuking Job so severely: He believed that if God spoke, He would condemn.

But oh, that God would speak,
And open His lips against you,
That He would show you the secrets of wis-
    dom!
For they would double your prudence.
Know therefore that God exacts from you
Less than your iniquity deserves (11:5-6).

Even when the Holy Spirit quickens the mind of the prophet, his concept of God will often color and contaminate the message. The censorship of the conscious mind will prevent the mouth from saying exactly what the Spirit is saying. Minor "corrections" are made to keep the message in harmony with the speaker's view of God.

I have heard my share of prophetic utterances that proclaimed a picture of God far from what I see in the Bible. When I later learned of the speaker's religious background, I understood how this had tinted the scene.

We see this illustrated throughout the Old Testament prophetic books. Isaiah grasped the holiness of God, and this view affected everything he saw and said throughout his book. Hosea, realizing the wonder of the forgiving love of God, highlighted everything he wrote with the rosy tint of God's love.

Since Zophar viewed God as retributive and judgmental, we could expect any message he gave to be colored by this conviction. Since Zophar's God was an eye-for-an-eye-and-a-tooth-for-a-tooth God, Job was just getting what was coming to him.

God chose to use these friends to enlarge Job's perception of Himself, but they could not speak beyond what they knew. Jesus, speaking to Nicodemus, said, "Are you the teacher of Israel, and do not know these things? Most assuredly, I say to you, We speak what We know and testify what We have seen" (John 3:10-11). Prophets need

61

to enlarge their knowledge of God continually lest their limited concepts restrict the communication God can share through them.

Rebuking in Prophecy
May Come Out of Prejudice

Why would a prophet with access to the wisdom of God call a righteous man wicked? The key may lie in the introduction given for these three men. We read, "Each one came from his own place" (2:11). While this undoubtedly refers to their homelands, it may also explain why they mixed God's words to Job with so much personal philosophy. Anytime a speaker mixes personal observations with God's message, he or she comes "from his own place." True prophecy comes from God's place — from His heart.

Zophar the Naamathite began his second speech:

> Therefore my anxious thoughts make me answer,
> Because of the turmoil within me (20:2).

He admits an emotional bias is motivating, and perhaps directing, his message.

Many sermons preached in the South before the Civil War would make one believe that God Himself was declaring that black people lacked souls and were less than human. How easily personal prejudice affects communication.

Parents know this principle of prejudicial conversation; sibling rivalry is reflected in the way children speak to one another. Even when communicating good things, many brothers speak in a derogatory way to their sisters, for example.

Bias and prejudice restrict not only the maturity of the person harboring them, but also (and equally) the effectiveness of any communication he or she may bring to the body of Christ. Instead of getting the full message, people will hear a condensed and slanted version. This was Job's situation. His messengers spoke out of bias.

Rebuking in Prophecy
Violates the Gift of Prophecy

Jude tells us that prophesying can be traced back to Enoch, the seventh generation from Adam (Jude 14). Yet the office of the prophet came on the scene after the Israelites rejected the direct voice of God, who had spoken to them from Mount Sinai. What God communicated from the mountain was a revelation of Himself, essential ethics that enabled the people to walk in a personal relationship with this self-revealing God.

The people told Moses that God's direct voice was too awesome and that no one could live through another such experience. They asked Moses to be their mediator by going up into the presence of God and bringing back His word to them. God accepted their rejection and made Moses the prophet to the nation. From that day on God spoke indirectly to His people through assorted persons and in diverse ways. These men and women are called prophets in the Bible.

Just as Christ has not commissioned all who can preach to be pastors, He has also not called all who can prophesy to be prophets. In the past few years much harm has come to the church because some Christians assumed that an ability was equal to an appointment.

Most of the prophetic word that encourages our Christian walk comes through the operation of the gift of prophecy. This is one of the manifestations of the Spirit as listed in 1 Corinthians 12. And Paul urged Christians, "Therefore, brethren, desire earnestly to prophesy..." (1 Corinthians 14:39).

This gift is not connected with an office in the church. Paul suggested that when the spirit of prophecy was present, "You can all prophesy one by one, that all may learn and all may be encouraged" (1 Corinthians 14:31). Prophecy is not inspiration in the same sense as the inspiration that produced our Bible. Prophecy is more of an anointed utterance; it is an enabling of the Holy Spirit to declare the things of God for the edifying of the whole congregation.

This vocal gift that flows through so many channels in the church seemed important enough to Paul that he devoted most of 1 Corinthians 14 to direct its operation. He said that prophecy was to be done in turn and judged by others (vv. 27,29). He lovingly reminded us that "the spirits of the prophets are subject to the prophets" (v. 32). He also said that this gift was especially valuable to believers (v. 22).

Perhaps the best wisdom he shared was, "But he who prophesies speaks edification and exhortation and comfort to men" (v. 3). This sets the parameters for the operation of this gift. God's Spirit speaks to edify, exhort and comfort. Reprimanding is not even implied in this list.

While pastoring together, Judson and I learned to reject messages that had strong condemnation in them. We observed that people often use the prophetic channel to project their own sense of guilt, conviction or anger. They often transfer a call of change to their own hearts as being a call of the Holy Spirit to the entire body of Christ. If they are prayerless, they often project their guilt upon the entire church in calling for more time to be spent in prayer.

The flow — the purpose — of prophecy is to edify, not to editorialize. God inspires people to exhort, not to excommunicate. The prophetic goal must be to comfort, not condemn. Job's comforters were out of order when they stepped beyond edification, exhortation and comfort — doing Job more harm than good. It caused Job to ignore correct prophetic teaching about God because of incorrect projection of guilt.

Rebuking in Prophecy
Ignores the Purpose of Suffering

All of Job's comforters assumed that Job's suffering was God's chastisement or judgment upon sin and iniquity. It is obvious that Zophar measured God's blessing in physical terms. He viewed poverty and illness as the fate of the wicked and health and wealth as the reward God gives to the righteous. He concluded his second speech, which described miseries and misfortunes in painful detail, by saying:

> This is the portion from God for a wicked
> man,
> The heritage appointed to him by God
> (20:29).

Each speaker seemed unable to see that seasons of suffering are often the center of God's will for a saint. These ancient wise men thought in terms of a life-span on earth. God thinks in terms of eternity, as He is preparing us for a much greater life, yet to come. They saw a superior life-style as evidence of God's blessing — completely overlooking that temporary suffering and privation may be tools used by God to form His own image in righteous people.

65

They did not have a revelation of the coming Christ who would be born to poverty, live an austere life and suffer at the hands of both believers and unbelievers. By the standards these comforters imposed upon Job, Jesus would have to be appraised as unrighteous and judged by God. In fact, that is exactly how the prophet Isaiah said Jesus would be viewed when he wrote:

> Surely He has borne our griefs
> And carried our sorrows;
> Yet we esteemed Him stricken,
> Smitten by God, and afflicted (Isaiah 53:4).

The author of Hebrews spoke very differently of Jesus when he wrote: "Though He was a Son, yet He learned obedience by the things which He suffered" (Hebrews 5:8). If it required suffering for Jesus to learn obedience, why should we expect to learn to obey without pain?

God called a person I knew well to the ministry when he was still in his teens. He went to Bible school to prepare himself, but when he married, he chose to try his hand in business. Though he prospered for many years in almost everything he put his hand to, he had great leanness of soul. Illegal business entanglements eventually brought him before the court and resulted in his imprisonment. In the state penitentiary, in the midst of great suffering, he gave himself to the service of the Lord without reservation. He now testifies that, hard as it was, the journey was worth the destination. Was this God's only way to bring him into the perfect will of God? No, but it was the easiest way he was willing to come.

In Paul's introduction to his second epistle to the saints in Corinth, he wrote: "Blessed be the God and Father of our Lord Jesus Christ, the Father of mercies and God of all comfort, who comforts us in all our tribulation, that we may be able to comfort those who are in any trouble, with the comfort with which we ourselves are comforted by God" (2 Corinthians 1:3-4). His word is one of comfort in tribulation, not deliverance from it. He viewed the many adversities that pressed upon him as being necessary. "For as the sufferings of Christ abound in us, so our consolation also abounds through Christ. Now if we are afflicted, it is for your consolation and salvation, which is effective for enduring the same sufferings which we also suffer" (2 Corinthians 1:5-6).

It is much easier to comfort one who has just buried a loved one if we, too, have undergone such sorrow. It is far more difficult to comfort and minister to the sick if we have never known sickness, for true compassion comes less by seeing and more from experiencing. This, of course, doesn't mean I must go through exactly the same disaster if I am to minister to others.

Paul did not feel that God singled him out especially for a ministry of suffering. He wrote,

> We are hard pressed on every side, yet not crushed; we are perplexed, but not in despair; persecuted, but not forsaken; struck down, but not destroyed — always carrying about in the body the dying of the Lord Jesus, that the life of Jesus also may be manifested in our body (2 Corinthians 4:8-10).

Zophar did not realize that what God had allowed to happen to Job was both for Job's sake and for the sake of millions of believers who would read of his experience in the years to come. He did not know that "our light affliction, which is but for a moment, is working for us a far more exceeding and eternal weight of glory" (2 Corinthians 4:17).

67

While it is true that God is a good God who does good things, sometimes we fail to see the eternal good because of temporal pain. Surgery never seems to feel good, but it is often lifesaving. Job was recovering from radical surgery, but his friends interpreted it as the judgment of God. May God continue to deliver us from such comforters or from becoming such comforters ourselves.

The story of Job may find its setting in the time of the patriarchs, but its message is as modern as color television. Why do the righteous suffer? — the accepted theme of the book — is still being asked, and we are still getting wrong answers. Many of today's messengers ("comforters") still seek the explanation in the life of the sufferer instead of in the sovereignty of God.

Rebuking in Prophecy May Bring
God's Disapproval on the Prophet

It is one thing to share a personal opinion with someone, but it is entirely different if we give it as a prophecy in the name of God. How often I have heard persons in a congregation stand and say, "Thus says the Lord..." and what follows is so obviously not of God that I wish someone would stand as God's mouthpiece to say, "I did not say that!"

God said through Jeremiah: " 'Behold, I am against the prophets,' says the Lord, 'who use their tongues and say, "He says" ' " (Jeremiah 23:31). Although Eliphaz, Bildad and Zophar all had true messages from and about God, they added their own thoughts to God's message and dared to speak on God's behalf. This brought them into conflict with God, for Jehovah requires honesty of His messengers. He wants those who speak on His behalf to say what He said and nothing more.

"And so it was, after the Lord had spoken these words

to Job, that the Lord said to Eliphaz the Temanite, 'My wrath is aroused against you and your two friends, for you have not spoken of Me what is right, as My servant Job has' " (42:7). God commanded them to take seven bulls and seven rams and offer them as a burnt offering. Then they were to ask Job to pray for them "lest I deal with you according to your folly; because you have not spoken of Me what is right, as My servant Job has" (42:8). It is dangerous to rebuke another in the name of God when God has not ordered it.

It is not clear whether Zophar had a third speech. Most likely he calmed down once he vocalized his anger and waited for Job to respond to his words. He had to be disappointed, for Job was just learning how to respond to prophecy.

SIX

REBUFFING PROPHECY

The book of Job abounds with dialogue. Seven speakers fill forty-two chapters with orations. God and Satan communicate. Then Job and his friends talk at length. Finally God talks to Job and his friends. At times it reminds me of a preachers' convention where everyone wants to share his latest sermon. Job was not only tested by loss of family, possessions, position and health, but this caucus tested Job with words. Endless words!

God did not give Job an open-book test. Job didn't have the answers in front of him. Worse yet, he didn't know where to find the solution, so he kept demanding that God share it with him. As God's silence lengthened, Job's tolerance got shorter. First he regretted having been born, then he wanted to die; toward the end we sense an anger in him that might have wanted the counselors to die. Enough is enough, even for a godly person. He wanted his friends to shut up and God to speak.

Consider the words of Job:

> Oh, that I might have my request,
> That God would grant me the thing that I
> long for! (6:8).

This was after Eliphaz's first speech in which he put Job in the hands of the Almighty.

Like many of us, Job was not able to see God in another person. In response to Eliphaz's second speech, he cried:

> Oh, that I knew where I might find Him,
> That I might come to His seat!
> I would present my case before Him,
> And fill my mouth with arguments.
> I would know the words which He would an-
>   swer me,
> And understand what He would say to me
>   (23:3-5).

It wasn't just Eliphaz whom Job couldn't hear. After Bildad spoke, Job was equally convinced that his friends and God were not really listening to him. He told Bildad:

> If I called and He answered me,
> I would not believe that He was listening to
>   my voice (9:16).

Everything Job had put his hope and trust in had been swept away. Now it seemed his friends were uninterested at their best and guilt-projecting at their worst.

He told Bildad:

> My soul loathes my life; I will give free
>   course to my complaint,
> I will speak in the bitterness of my soul.
> I will say to God, "Do not condemn me;
> Show me why You contend with me" (10:1-2).

Job is depressed and wants out! Victory never comes in mere abstinence. Christ is the victor and has become our victory. Paul said, "But thanks be to God, who gives us the victory through our Lord Jesus Christ" (1 Corinthians 15:57). Religious observance may prevent sinning, but it can also create depression. The upward gaze, not the inward look, always enables us to prevail. God does not call us to try. He enables us to triumph through Christ Jesus.

Job lost sight of this in his depressed state. He saw himself a victim when he thought of God. He said:

> I cry out to You, but You do not answer me;
> I stand up, and You regard me.
> But You have become cruel to me;
> With the strength of Your hand You oppose
>   me (30:20-21).

None of us can live victoriously when we see ourselves as victimized by God.

In responding to Zophar's word, Job could accept that God was wise, but then he returned to his original plea:

> But I would speak to the Almighty,
> And I desire to reason with God (13:3).

When all three of his friends had spoken at length, Job was still repeating his old plea:

> Oh, that I had one to hear me!
> Here is my mark.
> Oh, that the Almighty would answer me,
> That my Prosecutor had written a book!
>   (31:35).

By the time Job made this plea, Eliphaz, Bildad and Zophar had shared God's revelation with him, but Job had not heard the voice of God speaking through them.

Job had learned how to be spiritual when it was just "God and me," but now it was God, Eliphaz, Bildad, Zophar and Job. This patriarch could not sense the presence of God in other imperfect human spirits. There is something very special about a personal, intimate relationship with God, but there are times when God moves in His corporeal body on earth — the church.

We've discussed problems with the prophets' messages — the mixture of truth and error in any word that comes through the human channel. But let's look at some problems in Job's response to the word the Lord gave him.

Before I speak of Job, let me relate a recent experience of mine, ministering for a weekend at a church. When the pastor met me at the airport, he immediately expressed how important my coming to his church was at this time; neither he nor the church had heard anything from God for nearly two years. The church had been fasting and praying for God to speak to them through me.

After I got settled in my motel room, the pastor and his wife picked me up and took me to a fashionable restaurant. They both detailed the financial difficulties the church was experiencing. They felt they had to hear from God before the weekend was over. The story, with some repetition, consumed nearly three hours. Before we left I said, "You claim that God hasn't spoken to you in nearly two years, but tonight you have told of at least four occasions when God sent a messenger to you." When I reviewed those circumstances, they sat amazed.

"We didn't realize that was God speaking to us," they said. Like Job, they had predetermined the way God would speak and missed His message. Sadly, this couple is not unique. God doesn't always speak from a mountaintop or a burning bush. He spoke to Balaam through a donkey and to David through, Nabal's wife, Abigail, and the prophet Nathan.

The things Job's comforters shared with him were not what he wanted to hear, nor did they come to him the way he had anticipated. Job wanted God to speak to him directly; after all, wasn't he the most holy person in the group? You see, Job was not inherently a listener.

Used to being in leadership, his role was to impart knowledge to others far more than to receive knowledge from others. When his role in life changed so abruptly, Job found it difficult to listen. Like many of us, his mind-set compounded his problem.

Perhaps the format his friends used hindered Job from recognizing the voice of God. They did not proclaim themselves to be prophets, nor did they preface their communication with "The Lord would have you to know...." They just shared from their hearts, and the Spirit of the Lord joined in.

Job was not wrong in requesting direct communication from God. (God met Job's request at a later time and did speak directly to him.) This patriarch's problem was his insistence that God respond to him in familiar ways and his rejection of the unfamiliar ways. When Job rejected other channels of dialogue, he cut himself off from the information, inspiration, edification and comfort God had provided. God was not ready to answer Job's questions, but He was ready to reveal new measures of Himself to strengthen Job in the midst of his trial.

Job's Eye ("I") Trouble

Job had another problem. His steadfast trust in God was never in question, but his desire for an answer to his suffering kept him from the revelation God wanted to give.

Only the masochist seeks pain and trouble. The rest of us flee from it with a passion. Still, suffering is a part of life that few, if any, of us will escape completely. When it comes, we seldom face it squarely to see what may be learned from it. Our first response is: Why me? Why now? Why this?

God must be tired of hearing this word. I know many pastors wish the word had never been brought into the English language. When people come to me with their trials, they are not seeking answers to who or what caused the problem, nor do they want to know how long it will continue. They seldom ask a medical, social or financial question. They go directly to the theological inquiry — why?

"If God is such a good God, why...?"

"After all I've done for God, why...?"

"Why does my unsaved neighbor prosper, while I experience privation?"

The New King James Version translates James 5:11 as, "You have heard of the perseverance of Job." Few men or women in the Bible persevered harder than Job. He wanted God Himself to explain why these misfortunes had happened to such a godly person. He cried out:

I will say to God...
"Show me why You contend with me" (10:2).

God's response was indirect and was concerned with who had caused it rather than why it had been caused. Job wanted to know what God was doing, while Jehovah wanted Job to know who God was.

The cry of Job's heart was not for a revelation of the justice and dominion of God. He was locked into personal problems. He wanted specific answers to why his life had been turned upside down.

God was painting a revelation of Himself on the black canvas of Job's suffering, but most of the time Job tried to see himself on the canvas. He wanted answers to why he was suffering. Much of the time Job could see only the color being used at the moment. Like the hiker who was unable to see the forest because of the trees, Job so studied the brush strokes that he was unable to visualize the picture. He expected that anything God would say would focus on his innocence. He wanted a picture of himself, but God was painting a masterpiece of the Messiah. The words God sent to him were not what he expected to hear.

I can easily identify with Job. Sometimes God tells me things in which I have no interest, at least up to that point. I approach God with my list of questions, but He chooses to give me answers for which I lacked questions. God refuses to be bound to my agenda. When He speaks, He often prefers to talk of things of interest to Him rather than those things that seem important to me.

Most of Job's speeches involved and revolved around himself. Although he was righteous in the sight of God, he was equally self-righteous in his own eyes.

Furthermore, Job often didn't like what was said. He wanted them to talk about him and his difficulties — not God. Few people today want the prophet to speak of God. They so much want to hear about themselves.

When Judson and I were pastoring together, I stood one evening next to a prophet of God who was ministering to the members of our congregation. As he ministered over one couple, he spoke of the goodness and majesty of God in such a powerful way that chills ran up and down my spine. I was shocked to hear the wife interrupt the prophet, "I know all about God. I want to know something about our marriage."

Being a counselor to this couple, I was certain she did not know all that much about God, though she *was* well-acquainted with the problems in her marriage. She so wanted to hear the answer to her problem that she was missing the revelation that could have saved her marriage. She did not want the voice of a prophet but the mutterings of a fortune-teller.

Few things in life can prevent a revelation of God faster than I-centeredness. When the whole experience of life focuses on me, I miss every revelation of God.

Our generation has many impatient Jobs who travel thousands of miles to attend prophetic conferences so they can ask God why. They stand for hours in long lines awaiting their turn to approach the prophet, hoping to get specific answers from God. Their quest is not to know God. They want to know a *what* or a *why*.

The dependence of some persons on "getting a word from God" concerns me deeply. Some use prophets as spiritual gurus or fortune-tellers. When faced with a decision, they call upon recognized prophets and ask for guidance. What they receive is often a serious mixture of truth and error, which, if left unsorted, will lead the person out of God's will instead of into it.

I cannot count the number of times people have approached me in churches and conferences and asked if I could "get a word from God" for them on such and such an issue. In the mercy and grace of God, He sometimes gives specific answers. Other times the most I can do is bless the Lord and confer His blessing on the petitioner. Throughout the Bible the prophetic ministry frequently gave information, replies and specific instructions to individuals and nations. It still happens today, but this is the exception rather than the rule.

Even the Old Testament prophets acted more as representatives of God than ones who revealed the unknown. The prophets spoke to people on God's behalf far more than they spoke to God for the people. Each was a forth-teller more than a fore-teller, and never was the prophet a fortune-teller. Their ministry was to reveal God to the people by speaking His words to them.

SEVEN

RESPONDING TO PROPHECY

In Job 32 a fourth comforter speaks for the first time. Elihu is much younger than Job and his friends, and it seems he had sat quietly while the three older friends pressed their case against Job. But, listening carefully, Elihu had become emotionally involved. We read,

> So these three men ceased answering Job....
> Then the wrath of Elihu...was aroused against
> Job.... Also against his three friends...because
> they had found no answer, and yet had con-
> demned Job (32:1-3).

This young man was angry at both Job and the other three men: at Job because of his continual self-justification and at Eliphaz, Bildad and Zophar because they had not found the cause of Job's troubles while condemning him.

He began his speech by admitting his youth: "I am young in years, and you are very old" (32:6). While suggesting that "age should speak" (32:7), he also said:

> Great men are not always wise,
> Nor do the aged always understand justice (32:9).

He admitted that he was about to burst with emotion:

> For I am full of words;
> The spirit within me compels me.
> Indeed my belly is like wine that has no vent;
> It is ready to burst like new wineskins.
> I will speak, that I may find relief (32:18-20).

Convinced that what he was about to say had divine energy behind it, Elihu told Job, "Truly I am as your spokesman before God" (33:6). He felt that He was God's answer to Job's plea, and he began to speak of the grace of God and extol the God of grace.

The profound knowledge of God revealed in his speech seems to attest that a spirit of anointing rested upon him. He spoke more fully of Jehovah than the other three speakers put together.

Listen to a few of the declarations Elihu made about God:

> For God is greater than man (33:12).

> For God may speak in one way, or in another (33:14).

> For He restores to man His righteousness (33:26).

> Surely God will never do wickedly (34:12).

> Nor will the Almighty pervert justice (34:12).

> For His eyes are on the ways of man (34:21).

For He hears the cry of the afflicted (34:28).

Behold, God is mighty (36:5).

He is mighty in strength of understanding (36:5).

He does not withdraw His eyes from the
righteous (36:7).

Behold, God is exalted by His power (36:22).

Who teaches like Him? (36:22).

Behold, God is great, and we do not know
Him (36:26).

He does great things which we cannot comprehend (37:5).

Youthful Elihu possessed a timeless knowledge of God
that can come only from divine inspiration. Four times
Elihu spoke. Though he repeatedly challenged Job to
reply, this is the one counselor Job never answered.

Maybe Job felt he had given all the answers necessary; he may have resented such a youth speaking so
profoundly into his life. Perhaps Job was beginning to
realize that God speaks the way He chooses, not the
way we request. Maybe Job was beginning to realize
he did not know how to respond to prophecy — but he
was learning.

Listen Intently

Christians need to know how to respond to a prophetic
word — especially a prophecy directed toward a particu-

lar person. I have often observed people so overwhelmed with the personal word that they ceased to listen. Elihu pleaded with Job, "But please, Job, hear my speech, and listen to all my words" (33:1).

The very first step in responding to any prophetic utterance is to *listen.* How can we judge if we have not heard? How can we apply that to which we didn't listen? Through His prophets in Old Testament times God expressed His heartache:

> Because, when I called, you did not answer;
> When I spoke they did not hear (Isaiah
> 65:12; 66:4).

Through Jeremiah God said,

> I spoke to you, rising up early and speaking,
> but you did not hear, and I called you, but you
> did not answer (Jeremiah 7:13).

Listening is a developed discipline. As all parents can attest, few, if any, people are born with this capacity. Do you remember as a child hearing an adult say, "Listen to me when I am speaking!" A parent can tell by body language that a child's attention has wandered.

The same can happen when God speaks to us through the gift of prophecy. Perhaps a mannerism of the person speaking or a self-consciousness of being singled out in a congregation causes a mental block. An early statement may trigger a thought pattern that causes our minds to wander.

If we conscientiously believe that God speaks through prophecy, we need to train ourselves to listen intently. If the prophecy happened to be recorded, you can listen repeatedly until you comprehend the truth. If recording is not available, realize that you will hear it only once.

Listen up: Try to get it into your memory circuits immediately. Make notes as soon as possible after hearing it, as subsequent conversation with others will muddle much of what you heard. Just as the type-over feature of a computer erases a character for every entered character, so most of us replace a thought held lightly in memory with each new thought entertained.

Eight or more times Jesus said: "He who has ears to hear, let him hear!" (Matthew 11:15). If God gives the ability to speak His words, He will also give the capacity to hear them. This promise accompanied the coming of Christ: "Behold, a king will reign in righteousness.... And the ears of those who hear will listen" (Isaiah 32:1,3).

Listening to God, whatever the channel, strengthens our faith no matter what the existing problem may be. When God speaks, He may not answer our problem immediately, but He consistently reveals something more of Himself to us. We need this higher perspective and often are dependent upon the prophets to help us see from outside the furnace of affliction.

Jesus said, "My sheep hear My voice" (John 10:27). One contrast between lambs and mature sheep is this ability to hear the voice of the shepherd. Lambs tend to respond to any voice that calls, but mature sheep know the voice of the shepherd. New converts tend to respond to every voice that claims to be Jesus. More mature saints know the voice of the Lord, no matter what channel He may choose to speak through.

Listen Now — Praise Later

Elihu pleaded with Job a second time:

> If you have understanding, hear this;
> Listen to the sound of my words (34:16).

And:

> Bear with me a little, and I will show you
> That there are yet words to speak on God's
> behalf (36:2).

In spite of what seems to happen in social conversation, few people can simultaneously speak and listen (carefully) to another person. On far too many occasions I have observed people competing with a prophetic message by expressing their praise. Instead of listening to what God may be saying through this prophetic channel, they praise God loudly for His grace and kindness in speaking to them. Praise is always a proper response to God's voice, but it is both impolite and improper to interrupt God when He is speaking.

At a large gathering of Christian leaders, a national pastor from Japan knelt at a chair while other pastors prayed over him. As a pastor gave a prophetic word to him, he praised the Lord loudly and emotionally. The moderator of the conference pulled this man's ear lobe and shouted, "Shut up! God is speaking." Perhaps more such boldness in leadership would enhance the ministry of prophecy.

God does not speak to excite or thrill the listeners. His words give instruction and comfort. Our emotional reaction is only a by-product of prophecy.

Though we should listen before we praise, praise is appropriate. Every enlarged perception of God is a basis for an expansion of our praise, for we can never praise God any higher than our concept of God. As we let God teach us about Himself, it enables us to praise and worship Him more fully.

Respond to God, Not the Prophet

The divine order is listen now, praise later. Reflect, then respond. Congregations often applaud the message without ever responding to the message.

Job never responded vocally to Elihu. At the end of Elihu's last speech:

> Then the Lord answered Job out of the whirl-
> wind, and said:...
> "Now prepare yourself like a man;
> I will question you, and you shall answer
> Me" (38:1,3).

This principle is fundamental in learning how to respond to prophecy. Our response is to the One who sent the message, not the messenger through whom it came.

After giving a prophetic message to an individual, I am often plied with questions. The person wants to know, "What do you think this means?" "Why did you say that?" "Is the Lord suggesting...?"

It is unfair, and often dangerous, to assume that the person with the prophetic message also has the interpretation of that message. Daniel told King Nebuchadnezzar: "But there is a God in heaven who reveals secrets" (Daniel 2:28). It is far safer to go to God. When we listen with a calm spirit, we often discover that the Holy Spirit within us gives us understanding.

Although prophecy sometimes sounds cryptic, God gives understanding to the person to whom He is speaking. I have had God correct me severely through a prophetic word — while those around me thought God was praising me. The Holy Spirit within me was the decoder. While we respect the person God may speak through, our response must always be to God Himself.

Despise Neither the Prophet Nor the Prophecy

If, as we assume, Job sent for his friends to comfort him and help him to understand his afflictions, he must have been disappointed. While they had told him some wonderful things about Jehovah, they had consistently told Job he was to blame for his problems. Job could not accept this, for he refused to doubt his integrity. He asked:

> Should I lie concerning my right?
> My wound is incurable, though I am without
>   transgression (34:6).

Because these messengers mixed personal condemnation with divine revelation, Job despised both the messengers and the message. Instead of being comforted, he was confused. Although Eliphaz, Bildad, Zophar and Elihu were outstanding men of divine wisdom in their generation, they were imperfect channels for God's use.

God lacks perfect channels through which to communicate His word — unless He uses angels. Even the godly among us have human imperfections and weaknesses that affect the message God wants to send through them. When we fix our gaze on these deficiencies, we will fail to hear what God is saying. Elihu told Job:

> For God may speak in one way, or in an-
>   other,
> Yet man does not perceive it (33:14).

Even when God speaks in dreams or visions, we often question whether it was divine revelation or reaction to physical stimuli.

No channel of divine communication should be despised because of shortcomings. If I have my choice, I prefer my coffee served in a china cup and saucer. But I have enjoyed many cups of coffee sipped out of Styrofoam containers. It is the coffee, not the cup, that I want in the morning. Similarly, if I had my choice, all prophetic utterances given to me would come through supremely holy channels with no obvious human imperfections. But I do not have this choice. God has often spoken to me through an Eliphaz or a Bildad, and I have responded to the message. It is the message, not the messenger, that I so often need.

God will deal with the guilt in the speaker, and He has given some instructions for the hearer. Paul instructed the new converts in Thessalonica: "Do not despise prophecies" (1 Thessalonians 5:20). What you hear may be a mixture of what God is saying and what the speaker is thinking, but treat it as though you were eating fish: Eat the fish and spit out the bones. Isn't this what Paul meant when he told the new believers to "test all things; hold fast what is good" (1 Thessalonians 5:21)?

Like children who hear only what they choose to hear, many of us have developed selective listening habits. Sadly, what we prefer to hear is often not what we need to hear. Since God does not anticipate total purity in the channels He must speak through, He encourages the listeners to test everything they hear. The resident Spirit within us and the written Word are good touchstones upon which to test the purity of prophetic utterances.

My brother Judson had just been introduced as the evening speaker at a conference when a person stood up in the audience and gave a prophecy that said: "Listen to this man, my people. He is my chosen vessel. He is very special to my heart. He has come as a mediator between you and your God, so listen to him and receive his words as though I myself were here speaking."

This was too much for Judson. He thanked the person

for his high esteem, but he said, "We both know that wasn't God speaking, don't we?" Then Judson reminded the audience that God's infallible Word declares:

> For there is one God and one Mediator between God and men, the Man Christ Jesus (1 Timothy 2:5).

Whenever a prophetic utterance refutes, violates or contradicts the Bible, it is out of order.

Some people despise both prophets and prophecy on the grounds of imperfection. This makes about as much sense as not having electricity in the house because you want to prevent a possible shock. Because we need the energy provided by the electricity, we provide safeguards and education in its proper use. Similarly, we so need the spiritual energy brought by a word from God that we need to develop safeguards and learn how to respond safely.

Appropriate the Message by Faith

Jesus said, "It is the Spirit who gives life; the flesh profits nothing. The words that I speak to you are spirit, and they are life" (John 6:63). God's words to us, whether written or spoken, are life-giving. To be refreshed and restored, we need to respond to the life-giving words of the Lord — after we've skimmed off the unprofitable "flesh" that may be floating on the surface.

Jesus told the woman at Jacob's well,

> Whoever drinks of the water that I shall give him will never thirst. But the water that I shall give him will become in him a fountain of water springing up into everlasting life (John 4:14).

Watching flowing water may bring tranquility, and wading in it is refreshing, but drinking it brings life. It is the same with the words that God speaks. Just being around them can bring spiritual peace and invigoration, but we need to let those words have entrance to our inner nature if they are to bring life. We must learn to appropriate — drink — that word.

The door to our heart is faith. Only when a word from God is met by faith does it get into our inner nature and become sustaining life to us. I have often puzzled at people who have received a beautiful prophecy and yet remained unchanged. I have wondered how they could hear such directed communication and do nothing with it. This was the problem with Israel in her wilderness wanderings; the Israelites never lacked for a word from God, but they rarely brought that word into action. The New Testament says, "For indeed the gospel was preached to us as well as to them; but the word which they heard did not profit them, not being mixed with faith in those who heard it" (Hebrews 4:2).

God's spoken word must be accepted with faith. We cannot approach God without it: "But without faith it is impossible to please Him, for he who comes to God must believe that He is, and that He is a rewarder of those who diligently seek Him" (Hebrews 11:6). Faith enables us to reach beyond the natural realm into the spiritual realm. Faith replaces the natural fear the human soul feels in God's presence, and faith creates a positive response to what God is saying.

Referring to faith, I do not mean some mystical force that makes super saints of us. I refer to the simple, childlike trust and confidence in God that comes out of relationship with Him. Through experience a child develops a positive reliance on loving parents. Similarly we learn by being with Him that God is a good God who has determined good things for His children.

God requires that we mix faith with hearing His word, for He imparts faith in the hearing of that word. Paul assures us, "So then faith comes by hearing, and hearing by the word of God" (Romans 10:17). When God speaks, faith flows. We need but appropriate what He has imparted and use this to receive His message in our inner being.

Jesus told His disciples, "Now I tell you before it comes, that when it does come to pass, you may believe that I am He" (John 13:19). God shared advance information with His disciples so their faith would be deepened rather than destroyed when circumstances changed radically. I have slowly learned to let God choose the subject of conversation and join in with Him. I may not learn what I think I want to know, but I will learn what He wants me to know. It may well prove to be what I need to know to survive. God's ways have always proved to be superior to mine.

My years of walking with God allow me to look backward and see that the information God was sharing with me was essential to the ministry for which He was preparing me.

Obey Any Commands or Conditions

Obedience is another important response to prophecy. God does not speak to His children for the applause they may offer Him. He speaks to inform and direct us, and He expects to be obeyed. Elihu said to Job:

> He [God] does not withdraw His eyes from
>   the righteous....
> If they obey and serve Him,
> They shall spend their days in prosperity,
> And their years in pleasures.

But if they do not obey,
They shall perish by the sword,
And they shall die without knowledge (36:7,
    11-12).

God does not speak and then leave. He continues to observe the hearer. He seeks a submissive response that is unquestioning, unhesitating and unqualified. Our sovereign God is not to be bargained with. He is to be obeyed!

When I have not obeyed the last thing God spoke to me, even if He should speak to me again, He merely repeats His past command. God does not grant me the option to pick and choose what I will obey. If I misunderstand, He will repeat. If I rebel, He will chasten, but if I ignore Him, He may do something really drastic to get my full attention. God expects to be obeyed. The sooner we learn this, the more pleasant life will be.

After serving nearly ten years as associate pastor with my brother Judson, I accepted the pastorate when he resigned to give himself to a full-time traveling ministry. I was unprepared for the outside pressure that came against me and the church. It seemed that people could not handle a woman holding the office of a pastor.

Discouraged and confused, I accepted a business offer and left the ministry. I did well in the business, but I had extreme leanness of soul. When I explained to God that it really wasn't my fault I was out of the ministry, I received no response. When God did speak to my spirit, it was simply a reminder of His call on my life to the ministry.

Finally I re-entered the ministry, and almost immediately the Bible opened to me again and I could hear the voice of the Spirit communicating the truths of God to my heart. Until I returned in obedience to the last command of God to my heart, I could receive no further communication from God.

James said, "But be doers of the word, and not hearers only, deceiving yourselves" (James 1:22). It is not the mere hearing of the Word but the daily obedience to that Word that brings us into the paths of righteousness and blessing. Many people who seek a prophetic word from God would do themselves a favor by doing the last thing they heard God say to them before seeking another word to add to their list of accountability before God.

Obedience and faith work together like a hand in a glove. Faith causes us to know that God is "a rewarder of those who diligently seek Him" (Hebrews 11:6). Accordingly, obedience follows God's direction in full knowledge that good, not evil, will come of it. God does not speak to us to reduce us to the level of vassal slaves. He speaks to us to liberate us and bring us into the full liberty as children of God.

Please understand that obeying what God has commanded is not to be equated with trying to fulfill prophecy for God. The purpose of prophecy is not to position us to make God look good. If God says He will do a thing, He will do it. We need not do it for Him. I have seen frustrated people who tried to fulfill what God said He would do. Our only responsibility is to meet any conditions He may have stated. Then we wait patiently for God to fulfill His word to us. David understood this, for he wrote:

> Commit your way to the Lord,
> Trust also in Him,
> And He shall bring it to pass (Psalm 37:5).

Once we have learned to listen intently, respond to God, appropriate the message by faith and obey any commands, our most difficult remaining task is to wait patiently for the fulfillment of what God has said. It is easy to assume that because God spoke today, it will be fulfilled by tomorrow. But He often tells us His purposes before beginning a process that may take years to complete. From the very beginning He graciously tells us some of the end so we will be willing to accept the process needed to produce the expected result. Besides, God is never in as big a hurry as we are. He approaches things from the perspective of eternity, while we see things in our limited time frame.

It is not God's inability that causes delays. He must often work on many diverse situations in a variety of persons to conform them to His perfect will. Since He will not violate any person's free moral agency, He must use persuasion, and some of us are very unyielding to divine pressure.

Our season of waiting need not be unprofitable. Are the years of schooling unprofitable to a student waiting for graduation? During the season of delay we can review and renew our steps for responding to prophecy. Perhaps an acronym for the word that Jesus used repeatedly will remind us of these steps in accepting prophecy. Jesus said, "He who has ears to hear, let him hear!" (Matthew 11:15). The four major steps to receiving prophecy are:

(1) Hearken
(2) Examine
(3) Accept
(4) Respond

By hearken I mean to listen with the inner ear — the heart.

By examine I mean to test it by the Spirit and the Word.

By accept I mean to hold tightly to what is pure and true.

By respond I mean to reach out by faith in believing action.

EIGHT

REVELATION FROM A WHIRLWIND

As Elihu got lost in his description of the power of the Almighty, he vividly described a thunderstorm — wind, hail, rain and lightning. His description is positive and accurate. Long before modern science could confirm it, Elihu declared thunderstorms and lightning beneficial — gifts of God and manifestations of His power. He told Job:

> He causes it to come,
> Whether for correction,
> Or for His land,
> Or for mercy (37:13).

Then this youngest speaker concluded his discourse by saying:

> He is excellent in power,
> In judgment and abundant justice;
> He does not oppress.
> Therefore men fear Him;
> He shows no partiality to any who are wise
> of heart (37:23-24).

This lesson, which Job did not attempt to refute, set the stage for God's appearance to Job in a whirlwind. Elihu's prophetic ministry so unveiled God in Job's eyes that it brought Job into God's presence. This is the highest ministry of prophecy. Prophetic ministry should not leave us with a self-consciousness or even a sin consciousness. Its highest use is to bring us into the presence of God.

Even a casual reader will sense that Elihu prepared the way for God to speak directly to Job. It is not until we turn our spirits toward God that our inner ear is attuned to His voice. Elihu's constant proclamation of God's goodness and grace and His almighty nature moved Job's vision from his problem to God's power. Job finally looked away from his misery to God's mercy, and God began to speak to him.

The Whirlwind

"Then the Lord answered Job out of the whirlwind" (38:1). The turbulent forces at work in a thunderstorm occasionally create a spinning wind that descends out of the cloud as a tornado or becomes a twisting vortex that grows to the size of a hurricane. The writer of this ancient poem had but one Hebrew word to describe any of these phenomena: a whirlwind.

Twenty-five verses of the Bible mention the whirlwind. The prophet Nahum wrote:

> The Lord has His way
> In the whirlwind and in the storm,
> And the clouds are the dust of His feet (Nahum 1:3b).

While writing this book, I was ministering in Atlanta during a stormy season. Tornadoes dropped out of thunderclouds and leveled houses, trees, churches and commercial buildings just north of the city. Nothing could withstand these whirlwinds. From what I saw on television, the devastated area looked like a war zone. Man seems puny compared to a twisting wind.

Solomon described the workings of fear and desolation as a whirlwind (Proverbs 1:27). Jeremiah spoke of God's judgment as a whirlwind (Jeremiah 25:32; 30:23); he spoke of its velocity in saying:

> Behold, a whirlwind of the Lord has gone
>   forth in fury —
> A violent whirlwind!
> It will fall violently on the head of the
>   wicked (Jeremiah 23:19).

Zechariah quoted God as saying, "But I scattered them with a whirlwind among all the nations which they had not known. Thus the land became desolate after them, so that no one passed through or returned; for they made the pleasant land desolate" (Zechariah 7:14). This reference might be compared to a divine whirlwind that has recently struck the American church. We have watched religious kingdoms collapse, congregations split or disintegrate, and key leaders be defrocked or imprisoned. The high popularity that Christianity enjoyed fifteen years ago has dissolved as the credibility of the church has crumbled in the eyes of the world.

The Revelation in the Whirlwind

Those who have experienced a tornado will testify that it is a frightening experience. They never forget its roar or its destructive power. A mighty whirlwind came out of Elihu's description of a thunderstorm, and out of this whirlwind came the voice of God. It had a profound effect upon Job.

While this may have been a first, it definitely was not the last time God revealed Himself in a whirlwind. Isaiah said:

> ...And with His chariots, like a whirlwind
> (66:15).

This fits the description of Elijah's translation into heaven:

> And it came to pass, when the Lord was about to take up Elijah into heaven by a whirlwind, that Elijah went with Elisha from Gilgal.... Then it happened, as they continued on and talked, that suddenly a chariot of fire appeared with horses of fire, and separated the two of them; and Elijah went up by a whirlwind into heaven (2 Kings 2:1,11).

While Elijah was transported into the presence of God in a whirlwind, God revealed Himself to Ezekiel in a whirlwind:

> Then I looked, and behold, a whirlwind was coming out of the north, a great cloud with raging fire engulfing itself; and brightness was all around it and radiating out of its midst like the color of amber, out of the midst of the fire (Ezekiel 1:4).

The four living creatures and the voice of God speaking to Ezekiel came out of this whirlwind.

When whirlwinds come to our spirits, we can flee in

terror or we can face them as Elijah and Ezekiel did. The very tornado that frightens us might transport us into God's presence, or perhaps there is a revelation of God in the midst of the whirlwind.

The very nature of the whirlwind prevents us from figuring it out. The tornado holds a mystery for our best-trained meteorologists, and the storms God sends into the lives of believers bewilder our theologians. While the teachers are seeking to explain the why of calamities and suffering, God is often trying to reveal the *who* behind it all. The energy in the nature of God is so overpowering that His approach to frail humanity has the effect of a fierce whirlwind, but it is not the wind that matters. It is the voice from within that wind. God was speaking to Job, and what He said was a revelation of the Almighty. Webster's dictionary defines *revelation* as "a disclosure or something disclosed as if by divine means."

From Genesis to Revelation God progressively unfolded this plan to reveal Himself to humanity. Whether it came directly or indirectly, God's voice was the consistent method of His self-revelation. In the Garden of Eden Adam had fellowship with the voice of God. One of the final statements in the Bible is: "And the Spirit and the bride say, 'Come!' And let him who hears say, 'Come!'" (Revelation 22:17). God is a speaking God, and when He talks it is often like a voice out of a whirlwind. Unless we have developed a spiritual sensitivity, we may well hear nothing but the roar of the tornado or react to the emotional turmoil this frightening experience can produce. God doesn't speak merely to stir us. He wants to reveal Himself to us.

The Communication in the Whirlwind

Job wanted to negotiate with Jehovah. He had pleaded:

> Then call, and I will answer;
> Or let me speak, then You respond to me
>   (13:22).

Finally God did call from the midst of the whirlwind. The first words Job heard were:

> Who is this who darkens counsel
> By words without knowledge?
> Now prepare yourself like a man;
> I will question you, and you shall answer
>   Me (38:2-3).

This is exactly what Job had been demanding. He had said:

> Oh, that I had one to hear me!
> Here is my mark.
> Oh, that the Almighty would answer me,
> That my Prosecutor had written a book!
>   (31:35).

One danger of faith-filled prayer is that sometimes we get what we want — though not as we had expected. In our immaturity we seek things that we cannot understand or appreciate.

With two brothers older and two younger than I, I was always in a position of competition. I wanted to do what they did, and I wanted to have what they had. I remember pleading with my parents for a Bible. I couldn't read, but I wanted to carry a Bible to church and Sunday school like my older brothers. Funds were scarce, but my pleas finally moved my parents to purchase me a white Bible. Besides meeting vanity needs, it proved to be totally impractical for a preschool girl. A picture book would have been better, but I had insisted on having a Bible, and that is what I got.

Over the course of more than thirty chapters Job had been demanding permission to speak directly to Jehovah. He got what he asked for — but was it what he wanted?

The Provocation in the Whirlwind

God spoke clearly from the whirlwind. Job had no difficulty hearing and understanding Jehovah. He did, however, have difficulty accepting the message. Job had requested a question and answer session with the Almighty. He got it! What he didn't expect was for God to do the questioning and challenge Job to supply the answers. This was the ancient, and still very effective, method of instruction.

Jehovah begins, "Who is this...?" "Where were you when...?" "Who determined...?" (38:2,4,5). Already Job's thoughts are spinning like the whirlwind. God challenged Job's insufficient knowledge. Earlier Job had mentally either lowered God to his level or sought to elevate himself to God's level. He had declared that he would talk to God "man to man." This is impossible, for:

> God is not a man, that He should lie,
> Nor a son of man, that He should repent.
> Has He said, and will He not do it?
> Or has He spoken, and will He not make it
>   good? (Numbers 23:19).

Before we mock Job for thinking he could bring God

down to his human level, we need to look around and see what is happening in our society today. Recently there has been a revival of an old heresy proclaiming "ye are gods." We are not gods and never will be. We are persons made by God and in His image. Neither is God you or I. He is the Lord God Almighty. We should never approach Him as His equal, nor dare we envision Him as an exalted human being.

To accommodate our thinking, God is often described in human terms. We speak of the hand of God, of God having eyes and of our sitting at His feet. These terms are illustrative but not literal. Totally unlike us, God has none of our human limitations. No person at his or her highest level of maturity can equal God in any aspect.

God's fundamental proclamation to Job was "not to think of himself more highly than he ought to think, but to think soberly, as God has dealt to each one a measure of faith" (Romans 12:3). While God can talk to us at our level, we are incapable of communicating with God at His level.

The Proclamation From the Whirlwind

God's first message to Job was a limited description of His sovereignty — in terms to which Job could relate but not respond. The Lord asked Job if he had attended the creation of the world or sung in the choir at the dedication ceremony:

> When the morning stars sang together,
> And all the sons of God shouted for joy?
> (38:7).

Jehovah quickly convinced Job that if he didn't understand the creation of the world, he most certainly lacked the strength and wisdom to direct God in ruling that world.

In developing the revelation of His sovereignty, God asked Job fifty-seven questions concerning more than thirty fields of science. He asked questions that even modern scientists cannot answer satisfactorily. Like the smart-aleck student sent to the blackboard and humiliated by a teacher asking questions far beyond the student's educational level, Job sat dumbfounded before God.

Each question God asked Job came as a flash of blinding light that brought a revelation of God and an education to Job. All of God's "hast thous" and "canst thous" became evidences of what God has done and can do.

In God's second speech He asked Job why he was willing to discredit God's justice to put himself in a favorable position:

> Would you indeed annul My judgment?
> Would you condemn Me that you may be
>   justified? (40:8).

Then He described two mighty creatures that are subject to their Creator's power. The vivid description of these creatures reveals God's masterful art in creation and His supreme lordship and control. In contrast, mankind can neither capture nor master them but has been reduced to terror in their presence:

> No one is so fierce that he would dare stir
>   him up.
> Who then is able to stand against Me?
>   (41:10).

God's message is that mankind fears these creatures and cannot control them. Why, then, would any human seek to control their Creator?

Job lacks an answer to this line of reasoning. Job is rebuked and reduced to his weak human level in God's sight. God can still ask questions for which we cannot find answers. Jehovah stands supreme, unchallenged and sovereign. When we cry in frustration, "I just don't understand God," we are telling more truth than we know.

The Explanation From the Whirlwind

I find it interesting that "the Lord answered Job out of the whirlwind." He didn't take Job out of the whirlwind — the stormy circumstances of his life. Throughout God's conversation with this patriarch, Job's problems remained the same. The whirlwind that had demolished his houses, slaughtered his children, seized his cattle and ruined his health was still blowing. God did not speak to the whirlwind. He spoke to Job "out of the whirlwind."

When the swirling winds seem to devastate our lives, our prayers are usually for redemption from the winds. Yet these very winds may be the vehicle that will bring the presence and power of God into our lives. God often speaks from the midst of our storms. If getting out is all we can think of, we will miss a fresh revelation of God.

From chapters 38 through 42 God spoke to Job from the heart of the whirlwind, but He never answered Job's big question of why. Instead God assured Job of His care, concern and inherent rightness. Job's concept of God had collapsed because it was too small. His problems began to evaporate when he realized the greatness of his God.

The book of Job, contrary to popular thought, does not set out to answer the problems of suffering. It proclaims a God so great that no answer is needed. If God tried to answer our whys, we could not comprehend His answers. Jehovah chose to debate with Job over His manner of judging the earth instead of disputing the justice of Job's case.

Two thousand years after the book of Job, Paul wrote, "But indeed I also count all things loss for the excellence of the knowledge of Christ Jesus my Lord, for whom I have suffered the loss of all things, and count them as rubbish, that I may gain Christ" (Philippians 3:8). It is more important to learn firsthand something great about God than to have our problems fixed.

As we mature in Christian living, we should progress from demanding answers from God to longing to know God, into whose hands we have committed our lives. If we come to know Him, we will love Him. When we love Him, we will trust Him. As we trust Him, we will obey Him without demanding an explanation for His commandments.

The Transformation in Job

No one can see a revelation of God in the whirlwind of life without being changed — for better or worse. God cannot be ignored. Job's first answer to the Lord was:

> Behold, I am vile;
> What shall I answer You?
> I lay my hand over my mouth.
> Once I have spoken, but I will not answer;
> Yes, twice, but I will proceed no further
>   (40:4-5).

God had not spoken of Job's vileness. He had but asked unanswerable questions that revealed His divine greatness. In contrast Job saw himself as worthless.

After God's second speech,

Then Job answered the Lord and said: "I
    know that You can do everything,
And that no purpose of Yours can be with-
    held from You.
You asked, 'Who is this who hides counsel
    without knowledge?'
Therefore I have uttered what I did not un-
    derstand,
Things too wonderful for me, which I did
    not know....
I have heard of You by the hearing of the ear,
But now my eye sees You.
Therefore I abhor myself,
And repent in dust and ashes (42:1-3, 5-6).

None of the comforters' accusations could bring Job to repentance, but God's self-revelation caused Job to abhor himself and repent in true humility. It is not so much the awareness of our sinfulness that brings us to repentance as it is the revelation of God's divine nature. Paul declared that "the goodness of God leads you to repentance" (Romans 2:4). Perhaps the prophets of doom may scare a few people into the kingdom of God, but God preferred to move Job to repentance by a revelation of divine goodness. He still does!

NINE

REAPING FROM PROPHECY

If we view the first chapter of the book of Job as a prologue that sets the stage for the drama, then we must consider the final chapter as an epilogue that shows us "he lived happily ever after." After all, the book is a poetic drama, not a tragedy. It is filled with pain, but it ends in pleasure. Confusion controlled Job for a season, but God's comfort prevailed in the end.

I am frequently comforted by a simple phrase that occurs throughout the Scriptures: "It came to pass." Thank God, nothing comes to stay. Trials, anxieties, fears and pressures "came to pass." When the burdens of life seem almost unbearable, I tell myself, This too shall pass.

This principle has nothing to do with our understanding or faith. It is simply an inflexible precept of life that works as faithfully as the law of gravity. From birth to death, life is a series of changes, bringing pain as well as joy. We need to learn to savor the good as well as endure the bad, because the presence of each is only temporary.

Though Job did not seem to understand the transitory nature of his circumstances, they still "came to pass." The testing was over when he responded to God's voice.

Would Job's ordeal have been shortened if he had been able to hear God's message through his comforters? We'll never know, but why else would God have given prophetic utterances through them? I can testify that my difficulty in hearing God's voice has often extended my negative circumstances. As in the burning bush and the long trumpet blast at Sinai, God does peculiar things to get our attention.

God's testings come to develop us — not to destroy us. Even at the height of Job's misery, while his friends cruelly condemned him, he testified:

> But He knows the way that I take;
> When He has tested me, I shall come forth
>   as gold (23:10).

Whatever faults we may find in Job, passivity was not one of them. He vehemently withstood his comforters' false accusations and just as fervently responded to God's rebuke. When God finished speaking to Job, the patriarch responded in repentance:

> Therefore I abhor myself,
> And repent in dust and ashes (42:6).

Job had learned to react positively to God's actions.

This active involvement with whatever God was doing in his life continued in Job during the restoration period. The epilogue details Job's repentance and briefly states seven further actions Job took to reap the benefits of God's word to him.

(1) He released his friends through forgiveness.
(2) He recognized God's acceptance.
(3) He restored fellowship with his family.
(4) He received gifts from others.

(5) He responded actively.

(6) He realized blessings of increase.

(7) He rewarded the family that God restored.

Job did not wait to see if God would fulfill what He had promised. He became a participant with God.

Job Released His Friends

So many of the promises of God demand activity on our part. It's as if God says, "I will if you will." Job's response was, "I'm ready. What shall I do?" Job prepared himself for God's blessing, but God surprised him by prompting him to bless his friends who had so unjustly and harshly condemned him. God told three of Job's four friends,

> Now therefore, take for yourselves seven bulls and seven rams, go to My servant Job, and offer up for yourselves a burnt offering; and My servant Job shall pray for you. For I will accept him, lest I deal with you according to your folly; because you have not spoken of Me what is right, as My servant Job has (42:8).

What a stinging rebuke this must have been to Eliphaz, Bildad and Zophar — being forced to realize that all their attempts to cause Job to repent came out of their own spirits and did not represent the heart and mind of God. They stood reproved by the very God they had sought to represent. (It seems that exempt Elihu pleased God acceptably with his words to Job.)

As far as we can tell from the story, nothing had yet changed for Job. Boils still covered his body, his acquaintances continued to reject him and poverty enveloped him. It seems almost incongruous that God wanted to restore the friends before restoring Job. God's sense of priorities always amazes me.

It does suggest, however, that God is more interested in restoring individuals to relationship with Himself than He is in restoring material blessings. God always works from an eternal perspective. God was angry with these three, but He wanted a restored fellowship, and the shedding of blood was the only answer to a broken relationship.

Fortunately for us, God is a God of mercy. As we have seen, Jehovah told them to bring abundant sacrifices for Job to offer unto Him. God said He would accept Job's prayer for his friends and would no longer hold them accountable for their harsh treatment of His servant.

It is not unusual for God to use the despised vessel as a channel of blessing to those who once disdained that vessel. In insisting that Job alone could offer these sacrifices, God was humbling the comforters and doing a work of healing in Job. God quickly involved Job in a ministry that would restore the brethren who had mistreated him. This is one reason Jesus taught: "But I say to you, love your enemies, bless those who curse you, do good to those who hate you, and pray for those who spitefully use you and persecute you" (Matthew 5:44).

It was God's will to restore all who had participated in this test, but it was not His will to restore them separately. They had interacted to bring forth God's purposes, however negative this had become. Now they would need to interact to be restored to God's blessing.

More important, it was imperative that Job forgive his friends. He had a just cause against them and could have held them accountable before God. Their restored relationship was dependent upon Job's release through forgiveness. Jesus said, "If you forgive the sins of any, they are forgiven them; if you retain the sins of any, they are retained" (John 20:23). Job needed to release these friends to the grace and mercy of God.

Job had just repented to God, and he expected forgiveness. Now he was learning that forgiving others is a condition for being forgiven. How conveniently we overlook the words of Jesus: "But if you do not forgive men their trespasses, neither will your Father forgive your trespasses" (Matthew 6:15). Oftentimes prophetic truths spoken are unable to mature in our lives because of an unforgiving spirit. Jesus said the Word is like seed sown. The condition of the soil determines whether there will be a harvest. Forgiving others, no matter how seriously they have wronged us, softens our hearts to "receive with meekness the implanted word, which is able to save your souls" (James 1:21).

How easy it would have been for vindicated Job to write off his comforters as false brethren. In being an agent in restoring them to the grace of God, Job restored them to the level of friendship they had previously enjoyed.

Life is too short for us to make enemies of our friends. The word of the Lord comes to us along with sufficient grace and mercy to restore relationships — as we share with others what we have received from the Lord. Peter stated this principle when he told a lame man, "Silver and gold I do not have, but what I do have I give you: In the name of Jesus Christ of Nazareth, rise up and walk" (Acts 3:6). If we have received an authority, grace or ministry, it is ours to share. Mercy obtained should be mercy extended.

God's word restored Job, and because of that word he willingly restored his friends. Maybe we need less emphasis on religious structure and more emphasis on hearing the voice of God. His voice is creative. His voice is redemptive. The word of the Lord restores.

"And the Lord restored Job's losses when he prayed for his friends" (42:10). This is a cause-effect relationship. When Job forgave, God restored.

Although it is not stated specifically, it seems obvious that Job's health was restored — as the loss of Job's health was Satan's final blow against him.

No one anointed Job with oil. His comforters did not pray for his healing. God did not thunder from heaven, "Be healed, Job!" Job was healed by hearing God speak. This was the testimony of the psalmist who chronicled the merciful dealings of God with Israel during her wanderings in the wilderness:

> He sent His word and healed them,
> And delivered them from their destructions
> (Psalm 107:20).

God is a God of variety who refuses to be kept in a box of religious ritual.

There is more power to heal in one word from God than in all the medicines in a pharmacy. The four Gospels are sprinkled with accounts of Jesus' speaking a word that cured leprosy, opened blinded eyes, unstopped deaf ears and even raised the dead. It was not the faith of these individuals that healed, for nothing happened until Jesus spoke. It was receiving a word from God in faith that produced such dramatic physical changes. It still does!

Job Recognized God's Acceptance

"So Eliphaz the Temanite and Bildad the Shuhite and Zophar the Naamathite went and did as the Lord commanded them; for the Lord had accepted Job" (42:9). The King James Version puts that last phrase, "The Lord also accepted Job." Whether that acceptance was the cause of

110

the three men's obedience or the result of it, one thing is certain — God accepted Job. He had finished the test with more than a passing grade. This divine acceptance was obvious to the friends, but, more important, it was evident to Job as well.

God intends that repentance be a positive force. It is a way for us to start over without having to carry the penalty for past failures. Sometimes, however, we treat repentance negatively. We become so introspective that in spite of our righteousness, in spite of our words of repentance and change of behavior, we continue to live with a depreciated self-image.

The enemy knows how easy it is for us to feel guilty by accusation — by self or others — without being guilty of improper action.

Rose Marie came in for counseling looking like a whipped puppy. Her body language — her walk and her slouched position in the chair — signaled a poor self-image. In the early moments of the session a fountain of self-depreciation erupted from her. She claimed she was a poor manager of life's duties and a lousy, unfit wife. Her words were convincing; she believed her story.

In the weeks that followed I came to know Rose Marie through church activities. What she had said about herself could not have been further from the truth. She demonstrated good capabilities, and her children proved that she was a dedicated and capable mother. But I discovered that for several years her husband and mother-in-law had verbally criticized her every action. She had come to believe them. I encouraged the church women to give her an abundance of positive input, but any change was minor and temporary.

One morning during our prayer time the Holy Spirit spoke a prophetic word to Rose Marie through our church secretary, telling her how He viewed her. God assured her that He had accepted her in His love and that He was guiding her in raising her children. This one prophetic message did more to restore her self-image than all our month-long, positive input. Convinced that God accepted her just as she was, she began to accept herself. The change was soon dramatic.

Satan knows how well accusation works. That's why he has so many agents to assist him — filling our minds with negative thoughts and attitudes about ourselves. God's answer to this is to speak to us and to let us know what He thinks of us. Our self-image takes a giant step toward self-approval when God's Word speaks into our hearts, saying:

> The Lord your God in your midst,
> The Mighty One, will save;
> He will rejoice over you with gladness,
> He will quiet you in His love,
> He will rejoice over you with singing
> (Zephaniah 3:17).

Think back over Job's story and consider that God never used the descriptive phrases and titles that Job's comforters used of him. Even when speaking to Satan, God referred to Job as "My servant." That's what God calls Job again in the epilogue.

God sees His people differently from how they see one another. The promise is, "To him who overcomes...I will give him a white stone, and on the stone a new name written which no one knows except him who receives it" (Revelation 2:17). We need this change of character not only in the sweet by-and-by but also in the nasty here-and-now. Overcoming life's trials qualifies us for a name change.

People, even our friends, mark us by reputation, action

or failure. When referring to us, they may say, "Oh, I remember her. She's a divorcee." Or, "Yea, I know him. He was an alcoholic for years." These name tags, which seem written in indelible ink, do not allow for the work of grace God performed at Calvary. When God changes our natures, He also changes our names. He loves to tell the world and the devil, "Have you considered My servant?"

God still desires to change our natures so that others will recognize we are not what we once were. He is still in the business of giving us new names. He changed Jacob's name from "supplanter" to "the God-ruled one," and He changed Job's title from "sufferer" to "servant."

When Job saw God respond to the sacrifices he offered for his friends, he knew he was in right standing before God. He accepted God's appraisal of himself. His friends had evaluated him too low, while Job had esteemed himself too highly. Now Job could look away from both estimates and accept God's appraisal. If a prophetic word given is ever to be fulfilled in our lives, we must learn to believe what God says about us. We need to embrace "that He loved us and sent His Son to be the propitiation for our sins" (1 John 4:10) and that "He has made us accepted in the Beloved" (Ephesians 1:6). If we cannot acknowledge that God loves and accepts us, how can we believe He will fulfill a prophetic word He has spoken to us?

A false sense of unworthiness will cancel our faith, as it focuses our attention upon our negatives rather than on His promises. Paul realized this, for he told the Roman church: "There is therefore now no condemnation to those who are in Christ Jesus, who do not walk according to the flesh, but according to the Spirit" (Romans 8:1). Confessed sin is forgiven sin, and even God cannot condemn us for something He has forgiven. To reap the benefits of prophecy, we need to recognize God's acceptance of our feeble submission to His will and walk as forgiven and accepted individuals. Prophecy is not fulfilled because we deserve it but because God has purposed this for our lives. If He said it, that settles it. Believe it and walk in it. While still in tribulation, Job testified:

> I have not departed from the commandment
>   of His lips;
> I have treasured the words of His mouth
> More than my necessary food (23:12).

This is a healthy way to await the fulfillment of God's word to your life. Review, treasure and devour repeatedly what He said. This keeps it alive in you while it takes root and develops.

Job Restored Fellowship With His Family

Job lived in a day when relationships were more important than riches. The loss of the respect and fellowship of his family and friends plus the physical loss of his children must have caused the greatest pain in Job's suffering. He had been the patriarch of his clan, but when circumstances turned against him, even his wife shunned him.

When God began to fulfill His word, Job's third action in cooperation with God was to restore these broken familial relationships. Job declared:

> I know that You can do everything,
> And that no purpose of Yours can be with-
>   held from You (42:2).

He believed that God had ordained family relationships, and he expected them to be restored.

114

> Then all his brothers, all his sisters, and all
> those who had been his acquaintances before,
> came to him and ate food with him in his
> house; and they consoled him and comforted
> him for all the adversity that the Lord had
> brought upon him (42:11).

When opportunity presented itself, Job had to be responsive to reconciliation. He had to forgive past actions. He had to blot out of his mind the unkind words his family had spoken to and about him.

This restoration could not be done entirely from God's side. Job had to be cooperative. It is likely that he initiated the responses by reaching out to his family. Once he realized everything had been done at the direction of God, he could easily forgive the family for not understanding, for he himself had not understood what was happening to him.

A sense of self-righteousness or a spirit of unforgiveness can prevent a family reunion. The issue should never be whether they treated us justly or unjustly. The issue should be to try to maintain family fellowship. As God restores our house and food, broken relationships can be mended by sharing such blessings with our intimate family and with our larger family in the household of God. Job's family ate at his table. God blesses us to bless others through us, and that reconciliation should start in our immediate household. If we can't believe God for restoration in our immediate circumstances, what chance have we to believe the prophetic word of God for the larger situation?

Job Received Gifts From Others

Job, "the greatest of all the people of the East" (1:3),

115

was reduced to such poverty that he sat on a pile of ashes in an open field. Poverty is always unpleasant, but it is especially distasteful to people who have lived in luxury. Job, who once had it all, would have filed for bankruptcy if he were living in our generation.

When the word of the Lord came to Job, his circumstances were reversed. When the family followed Job's lead for restored fellowship, "They consoled him and comforted him for all the adversity that the Lord had brought upon him. Each one gave him a piece of silver and each a ring of gold" (42:11). The restoration process began through his family and friends. The mockers became comforters, and their gifts set Job back onto the road to financial recovery. What a picture of the body of Christ ministering to brothers and sisters who have met financial disaster and subsequently received a word from the Lord!

There's another marvelous twist. Those with whom Job shared out of his restoration became channels for sharing gifts with him. Like Rebekah, who rode to her bridegroom on the very camels she had watered, we often receive from the persons with whom we have shared.

Jesus told His disciples, "Give, and it will be given to you: good measure, pressed down, shaken together, and running over will be put into your bosom. For with the same measure that you use, it will be measured back to you" (Luke 6:38). The King James Version reads, "...shall men give into your bosom."

God allows the blessed to become blessers. Job gave to his family, and his family gave to him. He offered them acceptance and love, and they consoled, comforted and shared material blessings with him. The potential problem here was Job's willingness to receive from his family. He had earlier boasted how he had cared for his family and even for strangers. Now he must humble himself to receive from their hands.

God does not bestow all His spiritual gifts directly. He often sends them through the generosity of others. Songs, sermons, prayers or even written notes have often been spiritual rings of gold and pieces of silver to one who has been impoverished spiritually. Often these gifts come from others whom we view as far beneath our spiritual level.

If we are going to let God fulfill His prophetic word to restore us to spiritual strength, it should not matter whose hand shares with us. The gift comes from God, for "every good gift and every perfect gift is from above, and comes down from the Father of lights, with whom there is no variation or shadow of turning" (James 1:17). Job was willing to let God supply his need through any channel of divine choosing — even family members. Sometimes God still meets spiritual needs through a husband or a wife if we can humble ourselves to receive it. If we get too exclusive about who can bless us, we may miss the fulfillment of God's prophetic word to our lives.

Job Responded Actively

The epilogue says, "And the Lord restored Job's losses when he prayed for his friends. Indeed the Lord gave Job twice as much as he had before" (42:10). The narrative suggests that God did not restore Job's losses all at once. It was progressive and extended over a period of time. It is likely that this praying for his friends was also progressive.

There are things God declares He will do that He fulfills in a moment of time. Other things take much longer to come to pass. If, as Jesus taught, God's Word to us is a seed that must take root, grow and mature before we can reap a harvest, then that word needs constant attention during the growing season. Whatever conditions God may have established at the beginning will continue to the end. God told Job to pray for his friends, and it is likely he continued to pray for them for many years.

How easily discouraged we become when we do what God requires of us and do not see immediate results. We must learn that progressive obedience brings progressive provision. God need not send His Spirit each day to remind us to pray, read the Word and share our substance for His work. We should continue doing the last thing He told us to do until He gives us different orders. If we expect continuity in God's fulfillment of His word to us, certainly He has a right to expect constancy in our obedience to the conditions He established.

Job prayed, and God began his restoration. Job continued to pray for his friends, and God continued to restore his lost resources. This concern for the spiritual well-being of his friends kept Job from introverted selfishness. It will do the same for us. God wants to move us from an I-consciousness to an us-awareness. The family of God is bigger than any individual.

Job Realized Blessings of Increase

Having actively participated with God in forgiving his friends, recognizing God's acceptance, restoring fellowship with his family and receiving gifts from others, Job ultimately recovered more than he had lost. We read: "Now the Lord blessed the latter days of Job more than his beginning; for he had fourteen thousand sheep, six thousand camels, one thousand yoke of oxen, and one thousand female donkeys" (42:12). This is double the inventory given in Job 1:3. (It seems that God prefers to multiply rather than add.) Paul's doxology still rings true: "Now to Him who is able to do exceedingly abundantly above all that we ask or think, according to the power that works in us" (Ephesians 3:20).

I can testify to having been reduced to absolutely nothing under the hand of God. When God's word came to me and I responded, God restored far more than I had lost. The creative word of God brings into being things that did not exist before He spoke. Paul told Timothy to "command those who are rich in this present age not to be haughty, nor to trust in uncertain riches but in the living God, who gives us richly all things to enjoy" (1 Timothy 6:17). The word of the Lord still restores those things that the locust, the cankerworm and the caterpillar have devoured (Joel 2:25).

Job reaped bountifully from the promises God had given him. When he surrendered to God's point of view, God rebuked the power of Satan over his life and gave back double for all that he had lost. His harvest was not in eternity. It was in time and on the earth. God resides in an eternal now. His promises affect both His now and our present. When God speaks, His word is accomplished, but it often takes time for Him to adjust us to receive what He has purposed for us.

We dare not lose sight of the victory promised while we are in the thick of battle. Paul, pressed on every side, wrote: "And let us not grow weary while doing good, for in due season we shall reap if we do not lose heart" (Galatians 6:9).

Job Rewarded the Family That God Restored

At the beginning of this sacred poem we read, "And seven sons and three daughters were born to him" (1:2). We know that all Job's children perished in the early attack of the enemy. But at the end of the story, after Job was able to hear God's voice, "He also had seven sons and three daughters" (42:13). God replaced Job's family person for person.

God's word restored Job's family. God views the family unit as sacred. It is not His will that the enemy succeed in destroying that unit. One need not be a prophet to recognize there are enemy forces at work seeking to destroy families one person at a time. Even godly people and full-time Christian workers struggle to keep the family unit together in Christ Jesus. They are not always successful. The pain of having a child walk away from Christ to embrace the world system is almost unbearable, but it is often intensified by religious people who call for these parents to step out of Christian service because they "do not rule their families well."

How sad it is to sit in judgment before the final evidence has been presented. The promise of God's Word is:

> Train up a child in the way he should go,
> And when he is old he will not depart from
>   it (Proverbs 22:6).

How old is "old"? I have counseled many heartbroken parents whose children departed from faith in God when they went to college or after marriage. Nothing I could say could comfort them fully. On occasion, however, God shared a prophetic word to them promising that their children would indeed return to Him. What a dynamic change it made in these parents' lives. Instead of living in self-projected guilt, they lived in a divinely inspired hope. God, who cannot lie, kept His promise. Many of them had the joy of seeing their children return to Christ. Occasionally the return was after the death of the parents. Sometimes at the funeral itself they wept their way back to fellowship with the Lord Jesus Christ.

Family relationships can be restored by a word from God. Family unity can be reinstated by a word from God. Family love and trust can be revitalized by hearing God speak.

When God restored Job's family, Job shared God's goodness and blessings with them. We read:

> In all the land were found no women so beautiful as the daughters of Job; and their father gave them an inheritance among their brothers. After this Job lived one hundred and forty years, and saw his children and grandchildren for four generations (42:15-16).

Sharing an inheritance with daughters was rare — unless they had no brothers. But Job wanted his entire family to participate in God's great abundance. He continued to share the goodness of God with four generations. He was a caring, sharing father who knew that God could bring his family into the covenants He had made with him.

God's blessings do not come exclusively to individuals. We can, and should, share them with both our natural and our spiritual families.

TEN

Resolving to Prophesy

Many people feel that prophecy is an activity — a grace — given to other Christians but not to them. They yearn for this personal experience but feel it is a special gift exercised by only a special few. But Paul said, "For you can all prophesy one by one, that all may learn and all may be encouraged" (1 Corinthians 14:31). According to Paul, where the spirit of prophecy is resident, anyone can exercise the faith to participate. It is not so much being moved upon by a forceful unction as it is believing in faith that God commissions the Holy Spirit to speak to and through the channels He indwells.

The problem is not inducing the Spirit to speak; it is in getting us to listen. God is always more eager to communicate with us than we are to talk with Him.

Some Christians wonder if prophecy was only part of the "good old days" in their past. That's how Job felt in the midst of his pain:

> Oh, that I were as in months past,
> As in the days when God watched over me
>   (29:2).

Job's remembrance of better days was not all bitter. While he was now the recipient of words spoken to him by his comforters, he well remembered when words of comfort, guidance, encouragement and direction had come from his own lips. He recalled the days when he spoke in the gates that:

> The voice of nobles was hushed,
> And their tongue stuck to the roof of their
>   mouth (29:10).

He asked his counselors:

> How have you counseled one who has no
>   wisdom?
> And how have you declared sound advice to
>   many? (26:3).

The obvious inference is that Job had once counseled in wisdom and given sound advice.

The spirit of prophecy had flowed through Job in the "good old days." And if we read closely we can see that Job could still speak forth wisdom given by the Lord:

> I will teach you about the hand of God;
> What is with the Almighty I will not conceal
>   (27:11).

Amazingly, none of the things that had befallen Job had destroyed the prophetic flow through him; suffering, privation and reversals do not affect the Holy Spirit, the giver of prophecy.

True, much of the prophecy spoken by Job was diluted and polluted with his strong defense of personal righteousness, but the things he said about God were true;

some of his declarations about the future had to be divine:

> For I know that my Redeemer lives,
> And He shall stand at last on the earth;
> And after my skin is destroyed, this I know,
> That in my flesh I shall see God (19:25-26).

By looking at a Gospel passage, let's review what prophecy is. Jesus said,

> However, when He, the Spirit of truth, has come, He will guide you into all truth; for He will not speak on His own authority, but whatever He hears He will speak; and He will tell you things to come. He will glorify Me, for He will take of what is Mine and declare it to you (John 16:13-14).

Here Jesus explains six important things about prophetic utterances.

(1) The author of prophecy is "the Spirit of truth." The pure, refined message of God's Spirit is always truth.

(2) The Spirit speaks to guide us into all truth. He is never the author of confusion, and His communication offers us guidance.

(3) The Holy Spirit speaks on divine authority; Jesus has commissioned Him to speak to us.

(4) He is a speaking Spirit who communicates what Jesus says. It is not a special grace for Him to speak to us. This is His mission to us.

(5) He will even share with us things about the future.

(6) He glorifies Jesus consistently. He neither glorifies Himself nor the persons to whom He is speaking. Jesus is central to everything the Spirit says.

In this passage Jesus is referring specifically to the

indwelling Spirit He promised to send after His ascension to the Father. This makes the ministry of prophecy available to every believer in whom the Spirit abides — whether or not the believer holds the office of a prophet.

With such an availability, believers should resolve to exercise this speaking ministry of the Holy Spirit. What comfort it affords. What wisdom it brings. It is a glorious source of guidance. We live far below our privileges in Christ when we fail to allow the Spirit to communicate the heart of God to our own hearts.

Prophecy is an inspired word from God to individuals. It may come through or to them from God's Word, by an inner voice or knowing or by way of a chosen messenger. That word may be to a large group of persons, both believers and unbelievers, or it may be directed to an individual, including oneself.

Prophecy Edifies and Exhorts

In his teaching on prophecy, Paul declared, "But he who prophesies speaks edification and exhortation and comfort to men" (1 Corinthians 14:3). As Job was exhorted by his friends, he, in turn, exhorted them. Some of it was very self-serving, and some of it was harsh, but Job entreated these men earnestly.

He reminded them,

> I also could speak as you do,
> If your soul were in my soul's place.
> I could heap up words against you,
> And shake my head at you;
> But I would strengthen you with my mouth,
> And the comfort of my lips would relieve
>   your grief (16:4-5).

He also told them:

> Your platitudes are proverbs of ashes,
> Your defenses are defenses of clay (13:12).

Whether exhorting his comforters or entreating his own spirit, Job entered the prophetic dimension of exhortation.

The New Testament strongly teaches us to exhort: "But exhort one another daily, while it is called 'Today,' lest any of you be hardened through the deceitfulness of sin" (Hebrews 3:13), and "Exhort, with all longsuffering and teaching" (2 Timothy 4:2). Paul placed exhortation among the gifts that we should stir up: "Having then gifts differing according to the grace that is given to us, let us use them: if prophecy, let us prophesy in proportion to our faith...he who exhorts, in exhortation" (Romans 12:6,8).

Happy are the Christians who, like David, can speak to their inner beings and say:

> Why are you cast down, O my soul?
> And why are you disquieted within me?
> Hope in God, for I shall yet praise Him
> For the help of His countenance (Psalm
> 42:5).

> O my soul, you have said to the Lord,
> "You are my Lord,
> My goodness is nothing apart from You"
> (Psalm 16:2).

> Bless the Lord, O my soul;
> And all that is within me, bless His holy
> name! (Psalm 103:1).

This is exhortation at its highest level. At times Job entered into it, and so can we. But in the midst of this trial Job was also learning to speak words of wisdom, comfort and exhortation to his own heart. He was doing that of which the psalmist testified:

> I call to remembrance my song in the night;
> I meditate within my heart,
> And my spirit makes diligent search (Psalm
> 77:6).

Whether or not Job understood the concept of prophecy as we speak of it today, he cherished the words God spoke to him. He said:

> I have not departed from the commandment
> of His lips;
> I have treasured the words of His mouth
> More than my necessary food (23:12).

Job had developed a communication with Jehovah long before these troubles overwhelmed him, and he could rehearse some of it in his memory circuits. A word from God need not be freshly spoken, for God is a God of the eternal now. The person, like Job, who has learned the secret of memorizing and meditating on the Word of God has a consistent source of comfort, instruction and guidance during times of stress and confusion.

But when we need a comforting word or an exhortation, we are frequently unable to reach deep within ourselves to bring it forth. But God has promised:

> Your ears shall hear a word behind you, say-
> ing,
> "This is the way, walk in it,"

> Whenever you turn to the right hand
> Or whenever you turn to the left (Isaiah
>   30:21).

When our memory circuits cannot declare the goodness of God, the indwelling Holy Spirit can and will. That voice we hear has prophetic implications; verbalizing that word is prophetic exhortation to our own lives.

My ministry requires me to travel thousands of miles each year. I spend much of my time away from home and alone. If I were totally dependent upon others to edify and build me up spiritually, I would surely perish. I have had to learn to appropriate the Word of God to my own life and edify myself by saying aloud those things that God says in my inner person. Just thinking or feeling these truths is encouraging, but I have found it strengthening to say them aloud. Vocalizing these truths reinforces them to my heart and mind. This is what Job was doing part of the time, and it is wise for believers to do it regularly.

What a delight it is to see Job exhorting himself to godliness, to continuance and to faith. Under what must have been an inspiration of the Holy Spirit, Job declared:

> But He knows the way that I take;
> When He has tested me, I shall come forth
>   as gold (23:10).

When pain and negative circumstances overwhelm the soul, we, too, need a quickened word that exhorts us to hold on a little longer.

One very effective way to edify and exhort ourselves, especially in the midst of painful experiences, is to sing unto the Lord. Sing His Word back to Him. Sing a "new song" unto the Lord, allowing the Holy Spirit to give both words and music. The prophets connected singing with the flow of prophecy. Elisha said, " 'But now bring me a musician.' And it happened, when the musician played, that the hand of the Lord came upon him" (2 Kings 3:15). These prophets knew there would be songs when God was among His people. One prophet wrote:

> The Lord your God in your midst,
> The Mighty One, will save;
> He will rejoice over you with gladness,
> He will quiet you in His love,
> He will rejoice over you with singing
> (Zephaniah 3:17).

If God is rejoicing over us with gladness and singing, it is most natural to join in prophetic singing unto Him.

Paul taught that the point of overflow of the indwelling Holy Spirit would be melodious. He wrote, "And do not be drunk with wine, in which is dissipation; but be filled with the Spirit, speaking to one another in psalms and hymns and spiritual songs, singing and making melody in your heart to the Lord" (Ephesians 5:18-19). When we allow the Holy Spirit to flow, we speak to one another in songs, and we sing and make melody unto the Lord. How often has my own heart been stirred to new faith and commitment by a song I heard the Spirit singing inwardly. When I joined Him in that song, I was exhorted to obedience and courage in action.

Prophecy Exalts God

Like Job, each of us needs to be edified and exhorted. This is one of the ministries of prophecy, but we equally need help in exalting God. The unnamed psalmist commanded:

> Exalt the Lord our God,
> And worship at His footstool; for He is holy....
> Exalt the Lord our God,
> And worship at His holy hill;
> For the Lord our God is holy (Psalm 99:5,9).

We also know it is a cry of the indwelling Holy Spirit, whose goal is to magnify God in our lives. It is difficult to exalt the Lord when we are examining our own misery. After God spoke to Job, this patriarch answered:

> I have heard of You by the hearing of the ear,
> But now my eye sees You (42:5).

God's spoken word became so powerful to Job that he mentally visualized God. It became more than an auditory experience. He actually recognized God's presence.

In the midst of his confusion Job could exalt the Lord his God. This flowed from the Spirit of God through Job. Job's human spirit was crying out complaints and pleading for death, but God's Spirit exalted Jehovah, whose hand was pressing so severely upon Job.

He declared:

> For destruction from God is a terror to me,
> And because of [but for] His magnificence I
>   could not endure (31:23).

His vision of the greatness of God gave Job the strength to endure. Job further said of God:

> But He is unique, and who can make Him
>   change?
> And whatever His soul desires, that He
>   does....

Therefore I am terrified at His presence;
When I consider this, I am afraid of Him
(23:13,15).

Out of this reverential awe of God, Job said:

By His Spirit He adorned the heavens (26:13).

Dominion and fear belong to Him;
He makes peace in His high places (25:2).

Whom I shall see for myself,
And my eyes shall behold, and not another.
How my heart yearns within me! (19:27).

While we lament our circumstances, the Spirit of
prophecy lauds God in high praises. As David cried:

I will praise You, O Lord my God, with all
my heart,
And I will glorify Your name forevermore
(Psalm 86:12).

I will praise You forever,
Because You have done it;
And in the presence of your saints
I will wait on Your name, for it is good
(Psalm 52:9).

I will declare Your name to My brethren;
In the midst of the congregation I will praise
You (Psalm 22:22).

These cries did not always come out of pleasant circumstances, but they were always the prophetic cry of the

Holy Spirit, who helped David look away from himself and his troubles to Jehovah, who was totally unchanged in spite of these troubles.

Even in our best times few of us really know how to exalt the Lord. We need the help of the Spirit, who knows God better than we will ever know Him. Also, the Spirit knows our natural limitations in expressing our deep love and adoration of God. Because of His help, many of us can testify with David:

> He has put a new song in my mouth —
> Praise to our God;
> Many will see it and fear,
> And will trust in the Lord (Psalm 40:3).

In light of this, it is only natural for Paul to say, "Therefore, brethren, desire earnestly to prophesy" (1 Corinthians 14:39). Using this flow of the Holy Spirit in our private devotions and daily experiences continually edifies us, lifting us into the presence of God and redirecting our thought patterns. Such prophecy exhorts us to continue in faith and love and to know that God is a sovereign Lord who holds us in the palm of His hand. This, in turn, directs us to exalt God with our whole heart and to magnify Him with all the saints.

This ministry of the Spirit is available, but it needs to be appropriated and activated. Believers need to resolve in their hearts to let the Holy Spirit speak to them directly and to guide them to Bible passages that will encourage and focus their lives on Jesus Christ their Lord.

ELEVEN

RESIDUALS IN PROPHECY

Television has expanded the meaning of the word *residual*. Its dictionary meaning is "a remaining group, part or trace." It refers to leavings, remains or residue. Residual is something that is left over. Television applies this word to the royalties paid to the writers and monies paid to the staff and actors when a program goes into reruns — usually a fraction of the rate paid for the original show. Rerunning a show can prove to be a constant source of income for shows that go into syndication. It is payment for past services that have present utility.

I see residual benefits in the prophetic word. No matter how profitable a word may be when it is given, a blessing lingers in the life of the person who embraced and applied God's word. God's correction or instruction is not short-term; each affects the course of life into eternity.

Some years ago God's word came to me and directed me to step out of the business world permanently and enter a traveling ministry. Obedience to this word created a pattern of life from which I dare not withdraw. It has changed my life-style, my method of ministry and my pattern of influence in the lives of others. It has not been necessary for God to repeat His instructions to me. Once

I obeyed them, God's will unfolded progressively.

The story of Job paints the same picture. God did not speak and leave him unchanged. God's voice forever enlarged Job's concepts of the Lord and permanently established his faith in Jehovah. The 140 years he lived after hearing God in the whirlwind were the most glorious years of his life. A word from God consistently lifts us to a higher spiritual plane.

The Prophetic Word Affects
Our Place in History

It is said that a man is known by the company he keeps. By this measurement Job was exceedingly noble, as he stepped into superb company after being tested and tempered by the word of the Lord. Before hearing from God he was a great man of the East; after he responded to God's word he became known worldwide. We never again hear of Eliphaz the Temanite, Bildad the Shuhite, Zophar the Naamathite or Elihu the Buzite, but we read about Job in the Old Testament writings of the major prophet Ezekiel and in the New Testament book of James. He lives on in Bible history, prophecy and exhortation.

When Ezekiel prophesied to the Hebrew captives in Babylon that Jerusalem would fall to Nebuchadnezzar, he said: " 'Though these three men, Noah, Daniel, and Job, were in it, they would deliver only themselves by their righteousness,' says the Lord God" (Ezekiel 14:14). Lest the Hebrews miss this message, Ezekiel wrote a second time: " 'Even though Noah, Daniel, and Job were in it, as I live,' says the Lord God, 'they would deliver neither son nor daughter; they would deliver only themselves by their righteousness' " (Ezekiel 14:20).

This is powerful company for the patriarch Job — and an enormous step from the ash heap. Noah was among the best-known of the ancient men of Israel; Daniel was a contemporary of Ezekiel and ruled with Nebuchadnezzar in Babylon.

Ezekiel catalogs the three men together by the common denominator of righteousness, which caught God's attention. Twice he said, "They would deliver only themselves by their righteousness."

David testified:

> For the Lord is righteous,
> He loves righteousness;
> His countenance beholds the upright (Psalm
>   11:7).

The Scriptures declare these three men to be righteous. Regarding Noah we read: "Then the Lord said to Noah, 'Come into the ark, you and all your household, because I have seen that you are righteous before Me in this generation' " (Genesis 7:1). Jealous politicians bent upon Daniel's destruction testified that "they could find no charge or fault, because he was faithful; nor was there any error or fault found in him" (Daniel 6:4). And the book of Job begins, "There was a man in the land of Uz, whose name was Job; and that man was blameless and upright, and one who feared God and shunned evil" (1:1).

These three men were outstandingly righteous in their generations, but they had another point of commonality: Each heard a word from God and obeyed it. Their righteousness may have arrested God's attention, but it was God's word to them that captured their attention. When God spoke to them, they acted on what they heard and they were changed. God recorded: "And Noah did according to all that the Lord commanded him" (Genesis 7:5). This was equally true of Daniel, and, by association, must have been the case in the life of Job after he responded to God's word.

The Prophetic Word Affects
Our Families and Loved Ones

The prophetic word changes not only the life of the person who embraces that word, but also the lives of those closely connected to him or her. Joshua's relationship with Moses changed Joshua; Elisha picked up a double portion of the anointing that rested upon Elijah. Blessed is the family whose father or mother recognizes and obeys the word of the Lord.

God spoke to Noah, and he believed and involved his entire family in obeying God by constructing and equipping an ark. "And Noah did according to all that the Lord commanded him" (Genesis 7:5). Because the family of Noah joined their father in this positive response to God's voice, they were all spared and became the seed that repopulated the entire world.

In stark contrast to this, Job lost all his children. Since Job made sacrifices and prayed for his children, some people believe they did not embrace their father's faith. Of course this is conjecture; all we know is that Job and his wife were the only family members who survived the tragedies.

If Noah's is a picture of a righteous family, Job's is a picture of a redeemed family. Initially the children were lost, but after Job embraced the word of the Lord to him, God restored the family. The book of Job ends by saying,

> Now the Lord blessed the latter days of Job more than his beginning.... In all the land were found no women so beautiful as the daughters of Job; and their father gave them an inheritance among their brothers. After this Job lived one hundred and forty years, and saw his children and grandchildren for four generations (42:12,15-16).

It is always preferable to bring the family along in righteousness. If, however, we get a late start or fail for other reasons, there is still hope for redemption and restoration. After the word of the Lord came to Job, his family was "born again." God offers the same hope to us: "Believe on the Lord Jesus Christ, and you will be saved, you and your household" (Acts 16:31).

The residual effects of obeying the prophetic word of God can span generations. In 1927 a clear word of God moved my father and mother from their dry-cleaning establishment in San Jose, California, into the ministry. They pioneered churches, pastored congregations, inspired others to enter the ministry and reared five children — four of whom are in full-time ministry, and the fifth is a loving servant of God. These children are the residuals of their obedience to God's word.

Just as Noah could not spare the world and Daniel could not spare a nation from God's judgment, so too Job could not exempt his children from calamity. Righteousness is not transferable, but it is available. Paul spoke of "the righteousness of God which is through faith in Jesus Christ to all and on all who believe..." and "David also describes the blessedness of the man to whom God imputes righteousness apart from works" (Romans 3:22; 4:6). Righteousness is receivable, but God is its only source. Even the children of godly parents must find their righteousness in a personal encounter with God.

The Prophetic Word Affects the Future

As we understand the Scriptures, there would be no human population on the earth if Noah had not obeyed the prophetic word from the Lord to build an ark, equip it, bring the animals into it and then enter it with his family. As valuable as this word was in enabling Noah and his family to escape the immediate judgment of the flood, that prophetic word was even more valuable for the future of humanity. The word that came to him spared humanity for another chance as residents on the earth.

Similarly, the words that came to Daniel reached far beyond his generation. God showed him kingdoms with world dominion, although they had not even come into existence in Daniel's day. This captive Hebrew saw into the events of our generation and, perhaps, beyond us.

God's word to Job took him back to the time of creation, spoke of present phenomena and projected his thoughts into the future. He may not have understood it all, but Job found that the word of God transformed his miserable present into a glorious future.

As a pastor I often marveled when a guest speaker with a prophetic gift would minister a word from the Lord to a member of my congregation. The prophet would speak of things in the person's past, clearly define problems of the present and tell God's will for the future. Because of my long-term relationship with the person receiving this message, I knew the accuracy of the spoken word. That one word affected the remaining life of the recipient. What a joy it was to watch that life take renewed courage with these fresh directions and blossom like a crocus pushing through the snow.

God is timeless, and so is His communication. He speaks of tomorrow as if it were here today. It is as easy for God to speak a prophetic word to us that will not be fulfilled for many years as it is for Him to tell us something about our past. When He speaks, whether through the Bible's written Word or through the spoken prophetic word, there is transforming power in the message: "For the word of God is living and powerful, and sharper than any two-edged sword, piercing even to the division of soul and spirit, and of joints and marrow, and is a discerner of the thoughts and intents of the heart" (Hebrews 4:12).

The Prophetic Word Affects
Our Concept of God

To the prophet Ezekiel, Noah, Daniel and Job were familiar characters who had been saved from overwhelming calamities because of their personal righteousness and their obedience to a word from God. It is improbable that they were the only persons to whom God was speaking. More likely, they were the most notable persons who were listening to God and willing to respond.

God is more eager to have relationship with us than we are to respond personally to Him. Jeremiah and other Old Testament prophets echo God's heart-cry:

> Therefore thus says the Lord God of hosts, the God of Israel: "I have spoken to them but they have not heard, and I have called to them but they have not answered" (Jeremiah 35:17).

> Call to Me, and I will answer you, and show you great and mighty things, which you do not know (Jeremiah 33:3).

It was these "great and mighty things" that God revealed to Job. The New Testament tells us: "You have heard of the perseverance of Job and seen the end intended by the Lord — that the Lord is very compassionate and merciful" (James 5:11). God's reason for Job's trials was to reveal Himself as "very compassionate and merciful." Self-revelation is always God's intention for an inspired word to people.

Job's comforters could not solve the riddle of Job's

suffering. The suffering they saw him endure violated their concepts of God. Believing that the truly righteous do not suffer, they reasoned that Job must have done something to violate his righteousness. Many misguided people believe similarly today, but pain and sorrow are not necessarily punishment or even chastisement. They are a part of living that God may override at His discretion or choose to use as a learning experience for the believer.

We live in a day of fresh inspiration and divine revelation. No revelation from God will violate the Bible; it will illuminate it. In His Word God has said much that our generation does not understand or appropriate, but each generation sees more clearly, as truth builds on truth — as Isaiah said it, "line upon line." Sometimes a prophetic word will open a person's spirit to the truths of the Scriptures as rapidly as turning on a light dispels darkness in a room.

God is a speaking God, and He longs to have a listening people. Like Job before us, many of us fear to respond to a prophetic word because it includes a mixture of truth and error. But just as we do not refuse to eat peas because we found a pebble among them, we dare not reject God's word to us because there is a foreign substance mixed into it. God can give us discerning hearts to recognize His voice as distinct from all other voices. We can, through the combined action of His Spirit and the written Word, "be diligent to present [ourselves] approved to God, a worker who does not need to be ashamed, rightly dividing the word of truth" (2 Timothy 2:15).

A deaf spiritual ear will produce a dull heart and a distorted image of God. Perhaps this explains why we read seven times in the book of Revelation: "If anyone has an ear, let him hear." Selah!